ACKNOWLEDGMENTS

Special thanks to Jerry Kalajian; David Richardson and Andrew Vallas; Peter Doyle; Brett Schreckengost; everyone at Humble Productions for their invaluable assistance; my wife, Kelly, and son, Julian; Bob and Stephanie Pick; Ray and Kathy for their support; my brother, Joe; Bill Adams; John Valentine; Nick Pileggi; Gus Russo; Al Guart; Brian Fischler; Kenny from Queens; Brian Rhodes; Dave "The Duke" Hill; Howard and everyone at the *Howard Stern Show*; Jerry Capeci; Dave Porter; John Capp; Ed McDonald; Scott from the FBI; Rob Stone; Michael and Gayle; Leslie Conliffe; Tommy Peters and Bill Correll; CPH Jr.; Priscilla Davis; Scott and Johnny Newman; Judy Decker; Shawn K. Waters; Calamari's Squid Row; Steven Bauer; Chris "Motorman" Robert; CarrieLynn Reinhard; Drew Ferrier; Tammi Land; Craig Ley; Scott Wartham; my spiritual adviser, Rabbi Mark; and especially anyone we forgot.

D1366306

A Goodfella's

GUIDE TO

NEW YORK

**Your Personal Tour Through the Mob's
Notorious Haunts, Hair-Raising Crime Scenes,
and Infamous Hot Spots**

Henry Hill

with BRYON SCHRECKENGOST

THREE RIVERS PRESS

NEW YORK

Published by Three Rivers Press, New York, New York.
Member of the Crown Publishing Group, a division of Random House, Inc.
www.randomhouse.com

THREE RIVERS PRESS and the Tugboat design are registered trademarks of Random House, Inc.

Printed in the United States of America

Interior Design by Melanie Haage
Maps by Michael Tanamachi
Interior Photos courtesy of Brett Schreckengost and Henry Hill

Library of Congress Cataloging-in-Publication Data
Hill, Henry.
    A goodfella's guide to New York : your personal tour through the mob's notorious haunts, hair-raising crime scenes, and infamous hot spots / Henry Hill; with Bryon Schreckengost.
      p.   cm.
    Includes index.
    ISBN 0-7615-1538-0
    1. New York (N.Y.)—Guidebooks. 2. Gangsters—Homes and haunts—New York (State)—New York—Guidebooks. 3. Organized crime—New York (State)—New York—History—Miscellanea. I. Schreckengost, Bryon. II. Title.
F128.18 .H525   2002
364.1'06'097471—dc21   2002155438

ISBN 0-7615-1538-0

10 9 8 7 6 5 4 3 2 1

First Edition

To the law enforcement agencies in the tri-state area who made this all possible and to Barbara Abegg for her intelligence and patience.

C O N T E N T S

INTRODUCTION

New York City. The world's greatest. Filled with beautiful parks, grand structures, the finest theatres, and historical landmarks. And mobsters. I was one of them. They made a little movie about us: *Goodfellas.* Check it out if you haven't seen it. You'll get my "point of view" then and now—because let me tell you, the mob still exists. Anyone that says it doesn't is either a schmuck or a gangster himself.

To this day, there isn't a street in New York where something mob-related isn't going on. Someone's cookin' the books, controlling the rent, or shaking someone down. The wiseguys are embedded in every form of commerce. From the fish markets to the stock market. Seeing a show at Carnegie Hall? In my day, those instruments didn't get lifted off the trucks and appear on stage unless someone got greased. Every foot of piping, every inch of wire, even the concrete you're walking on, has been taxed by the mob. They tax everything. Don't like it? Sorry, that's just the way it is.

The city is divided into five boroughs and five families. All the families do business in every borough. I'm going take you through each. I know the best places to eat, sleep, and drink. The spots wiseguys dine. The spots wiseguys die. Sometimes the same spot. We'll check out gravesites, the ones that are legit and the kind no one cuts the grass for. The famous mob hangouts and sites of famous mob shootouts, past and present. Faces and names may have changed, but the game's still the same. Tread lightly.

So as one of mine used to say, "Grab your sac and watch your back. . . ." I'm about to show you a New York you have never seen. My New York.

Just don't tell 'em I sent you.

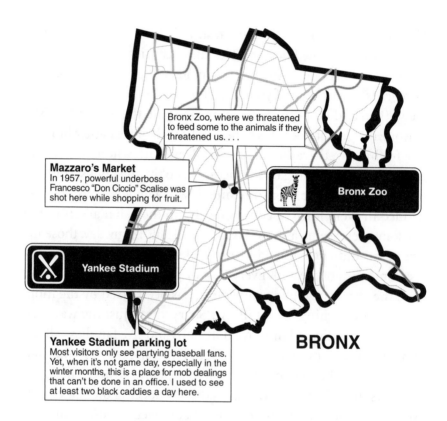

Bronx Zoo, where we threatened to feed some to the animals if they threatened us. . . .

Mazzaro's Market
In 1957, powerful underboss Francesco "Don Ciccio" Scalise was shot here while shopping for fruit.

Bronx Zoo

Yankee Stadium

BRONX

Yankee Stadium parking lot
Most visitors only see partying baseball fans. Yet, when it's not game day, especially in the winter months, this is a place for mob dealings that can't be done in an office. I used to see at least two black caddies a day here.

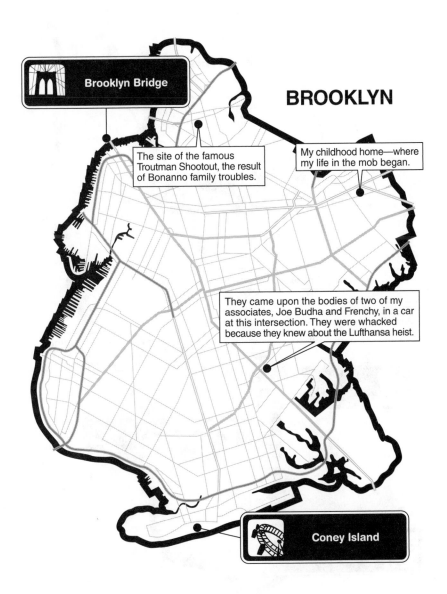

BROOKLYN

Brooklyn Bridge

The site of the famous Troutman Shootout, the result of Bonanno family troubles.

My childhood home—where my life in the mob began.

They came upon the bodies of two of my associates, Joe Budha and Frenchy, in a car at this intersection. They were whacked because they knew about the Lufthansa heist.

Coney Island

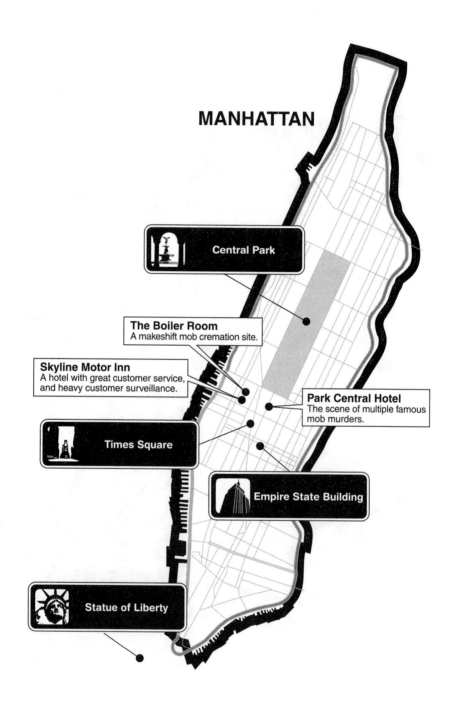

MANHATTAN

Central Park

The Boiler Room
A makeshift mob cremation site.

Skyline Motor Inn
A hotel with great customer service, and heavy customer surveillance.

Park Central Hotel
The scene of multiple famous mob murders.

Times Square

Empire State Building

Statue of Liberty

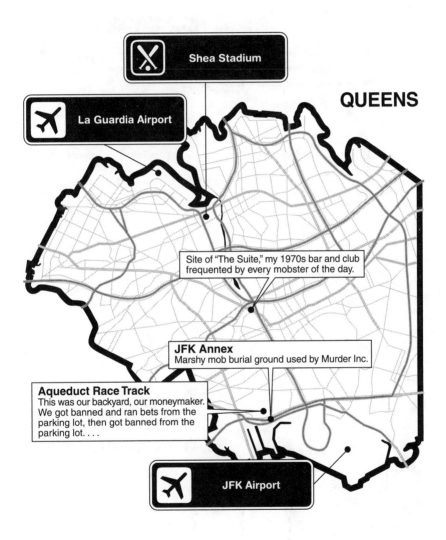

Shea Stadium

La Guardia Airport

QUEENS

Site of "The Suite," my 1970s bar and club frequented by every mobster of the day.

JFK Annex
Marshy mob burial ground used by Murder Inc.

Aqueduct Race Track
This was our backyard, our moneymaker. We got banned and ran bets from the parking lot, then got banned from the parking lot. . . .

JFK Airport

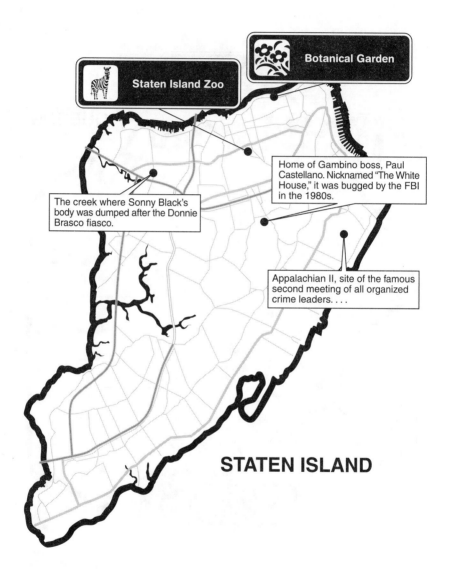

Staten Island Zoo

Botanical Garden

The creek where Sonny Black's body was dumped after the Donnie Brasco fiasco.

Home of Gambino boss, Paul Castellano. Nicknamed "The White House," it was bugged by the FBI in the 1980s.

Appalachian II, site of the famous second meeting of all organized crime leaders. . . .

STATEN ISLAND

The City

H ere's some shit you should know before we get started. The capital of New York State is Albany, the capital of the world is New York City. The state song is of course "I Love New York." Who wrote it? Don't worry about it. New York is the best city in the world. It's the only city in the world. New York never closes, at least for us guys. We run it from sunup to sundown and all times in between.

When most people think of New York, they think of the island of Manhattan. Originally named New Amsterdam by none other than the Dutch. History claims some jerk, Peter Minuit, bought it from the Native American inhabitants for about twenty-four bucks in worthless, weird crap. Hell, Peter could have worked for us. The only thing similar between New Amsterdam and Manhattan today is the prostitutes and the drugs (although neither are legalized here). Damn. New York got its present name in 1665 after those damn redcoats seized it from the Dutch. The pompous jerks renamed it in honor of their boyfriend, James the Duke of York, brother of King Charles II.

Why is it called the Big Apple, Henry? Conflicting reports. Some say back in the 1920s and 1930s, Jazz musicians used to refer to New York as the "Big Apple." Others claim that stable hands up from New Orleans had big aspirations and regarded the New York racetracks as the big show. Even some historian stiffs believe guys in suits sold apples for extra dough on the streets during the Great Depression. How stupid. I say who gives a shit. It's a big place and we always took a juicy bite out of it. Don't like it? Move to Nebraska.

The Boroughs

I was born in Brooklyn. It was originally a settlement called Brooklyn Ferry (hey, we used to call a guy that), back in 1816. By the mid-1800s it combined with Gravesend and Flatbush (no comment on this one) to form what is now known as Brooklyn.

Queens is not for queens. Historians point out it was once farmland. I'd like to point out that most cities used to be farmland. Farmland is a natural step in the settlement process, unless it's Vegas. (The late Bugsy Siegel pulled Vegas out of no-man's-land.) The 19th century brought immigrants to Queens to fill up the now densely populated residential community.

The Bronx is the only mainland borough. Initially populated with Irish and Italian immigrants, it is now full of all kinds of folks. Some guy in the 1600s with the last name of Bronck had his farm here. Bronck's farm. Get it?

Staten Island was officially owned (according to the conquerors) when the Dork, I mean Duke, of York wasted it as a prize to the winner of a sailing race. *Sailing,* for crying out loud. Those wusses never heard of poker? Lots of wiseguys lived and live out there in Staten Island, especially the higher-ups. They're close enough to the city but far enough away.

Manhattan is the skyscraping metropolis you see on all the postcards. It's where a huge chunk of the folks living in the other boroughs work. All five boroughs are connected by an elaborate subway system and bridges and tunnels. All five boroughs are "connected" in another way because, hey, it's New York City.

For everything you don't find in this book, which means most non–Mafia-related sights, there is one place I highly recommend you visit: The Official New York City Visitor Information Center on 810 Seventh Avenue, between 52nd and 53rd Streets (212-484-1222).

BOROUGHS STATISTICS

The five boroughs of New York City are some of the most populated areas in the world.

Approximate Population (Including Wiseguys)

Manhattan	1,600,000 residents
Bronx	1,200,000 residents
Brooklyn	2,300,000 residents
Queens	2,000,000 residents
Staten Island	400,000 residents

THE WEATHER AND THE SEASONS

New York City has five mob families and four seasons. Summers, with the humidity, are very hot and can be disgusting. Winters, with wind chill, are ball-chilling cold. Spring and autumn can be damp and lousy or sunny and spectacular.

Christmas is my favorite time of year. People are friendlier from December 1 to New Year's, and New York becomes a different city. The lights illuminate everybody. We used to make our best scores around Christmastime. Just check the papers, you'll see the biggest scores in New York City still happen in December. Hey, the families need their Christmas money. After the holidays and through Easter, a lot of guys head to Florida. They commute back and forth, sometimes even down to the islands, Puerto Rico and shit. Winters can get pretty miserable in New York.

Summers get so damn humid, a day hardly goes by you don't have swamp-ass by noon. Even with just my track shorts, it's impossible to stay cool in Brooklyn. Get out to the island. Those subways, oh my, the stale wet air. The street entrances to them become orifices of the city's ass. Even seasoned patrons of public transportation gag. I was hung over and puked on myself once heading back to Bay Ridge from 51st and Lex. What memories.

Average Temperatures

January	32°F	0°C
February	34°F	1°C
March	41°F	5°C
April	54°F	12°C
May	61°F	17°C
June	71°F	22°C
July	77°F	25°C
August	76°F	24°C
September	68°F	20°C
October	58°F	14°C
November	48°F	8°C
December	36°F	2°C

History of the New York Mob

The Mafia as we know it started in the 19th century in Sicily, when some of its families needed protection. Simple as that. My mom was from Sicily, and the mob didn't have a bad rap over there. The idea was landowners needed real and effective protection from invaders, and the government wouldn't give it to them. Of course the mob as we know it has grown from those simple beginnings, but it's still the same formula. All the Mafia really does is provide services and products and allow for methods of earnings the government doesn't. That's all.

New York was the perfect breeding ground for wiseguys. Spawned from the shitload of new government-weary immigrants that flooded the city from Europe, the American version of the Mafia was born. It was still about protection, even in New York.

Into the 1920s and '30s things got interesting and more organized. Manhattan was the hub of all the activity, and the mob got their fingers into every industry there was. Sanitation pickup, textiles, excise taxes, stagehands—nothing happens in New York even today without someone's hand out. The mob still has a payroll sheet full of city and state officials. Corrupt cops, referred to as "girlfriends," still roam the precincts.

Was there turf in those early days? Yeah, the families chopped the city up but not geographically. In 1931, mob boss Salvatore Maranzano created five families that were to report to him. His chosen leaders soon killed him, but the five families lived on. Their divisions were more the different families controlling specific services, not boroughs or neighborhoods. Usually, whoever got there first to claim it owned that service (until someone else came along and forced them out). There was always animosity and jealousy when families interacted. There just was. There were always sit-downs for beefs from someone banging another's girl to banging another member's brains in. Keeping it in the family saved a lot of killing, but there was no stopping it altogether. Interaction with the outside world was frowned upon. If you could, keep it in house. A lot less people die. Still, people got murdered. People died.

The Five Families

Mafia "family" is a romantic term for organized crime team or club. Strip away all the bullshit honor and rituals, and you're left with a successful team that's been around longer than the Yanks. The playing fields? The streets.

BONANNO

I knew a lot of these guys. I got along with everybody. Joe "Bananas" Bonanno (Bananas 'cause he was nuts) was the first boss of this household-name family. A bunch of shit went down in 1964 at his place on Park Avenue and 37th Street, while under a lot of underworld heat, a supposedly staged kidnapping. All the families were coming down on him following news Bonanno was planning a Godfather-like mass clipping. He wanted to be the only boss, and well, the other bosses didn't like it, so he got himself kidnapped. Colombo blew the whistle and took control of the Profaci family, renamed. The family was best known for its loan-sharking talents, but it dabbled in gambling, drugs, and other activities, too. Famous Underboss Carmine Galante would rise to the highest seat as well.

GAMBINO

The Gambinos are one hell of a family to reckon with. Publicized, organized, and glorified. Perhaps the most famous family because of John Gotti, Sammy "The Bull" Gravano, and Paul Castellano. Its former boss, Albert "The Mad Hatter" Anastasia, was maybe the most ruthless and famous wiseguy in wiseguy history. They called him the "Mad Hatter" because he wore these crazy fucking hats, and he was fucking crazy. Then there was Carlo Gambino, the legendary "Don Carlo," a small-framed but very powerful boss who lived to a ripe old age, somehow dying by the will of God and not the will of his enemies . . . or friends. Their vast earning areas include but aren't limited to: taxing and bootlegging gasoline, the labor rackets, trucking, construction, and gambling.

GENOVESE

Although it wasn't called such until Vito Genovese took over the reins in the mid-1950s, the Genovese family was born from the aftermath of the Castellammarse war, a 1930s battle between reigning mob bosses Maranzano and Masseria. (Both men hailed from the Castellammarese section of Sicily.) Prior to Vito Genovese, another infamous crime figure ruled, Frank Costello (no relation to Elvis). A more current name to reference would be the publicly-pajama-wearing boss, Vincent "The Chin" Gigante. He tried to prove insanity to the court by wandering the streets talking to himself, dressed in silk pajamas. I think anyone who lives this lifestyle is insane, period. The whole thing is insanity.

The Upper East Side to the right.
The most beautiful girls I have ever seen.

LUCCHESE

As far back as I can remember, the Luccheses were the most vicious family, a lot because of our crew, especially Jimmy Burke (Robert De Niro played his character in *Goodfellas*). This is the family of Tommy Lucchese, also considered the Fifth Family. This was the family I was involved with, although I was far from the upper ranks. I was an earner, and, believe me, we delved into almost anything that earned.

COLOMBO

Once the Profaci family, this became the now-famous Colombo family when Colombo himself took over. This powerhouse scared the shit out of everyone near them. Bosses like Persico and then his kid kept the family alive with a variety of hits, splits, and scores. Colombo ended up getting it at his own festival. Why? Keep reading.

Spotting the Mafia

The Mafia and its members come in all shapes and sizes. I think of it like watching birds; you can see the pecking order. The way people act around each other, in nightclubs or in the streets, you can just tell. Here's what to look for, and try not to stare.

The Boss is, the boss. If you see him out and walking about, or out to eat, he'll usually have a small, intimidating entourage. Look for a couple expressionless henchmen standing outside a restaurant, keeping an eye on a table inside. Chances are there may be a boss nearby. He has final yea or nay in all matters. Bosses are older than younger, have paid their dues to hell and back, and have been lucky (or unlucky) enough to survive this long, while keeping some sort of respect, and most important, *fear* from their associates.

The Consigliere is the highest, and sometimes only, legit advisor. Good luck finding this one. He may resemble a high-class seasoned lawyer or a low-class thug. He's a smart and influential underworld insider. You might see him in public with the boss. He has the boss's ear, and, a rarity, the boss's trust.

The Underboss is a VP of sorts and at times will get his hands a bit dirtier than the boss. These guys do spend some time outside, in the mix. They will have associates by their sides at all times. Being an underboss can be a death sentence or a stepping-stone to the big seat.

The Capos are the middlemen, sometimes called skippers. They are the connection between the streets and the office, between the earners and the earnings. They are always on the move, always giving orders and checking up on soldiers and their operations, often over a meal.

Soldiers are your stereotypical "wiseguys." They're the ones out there on the street swindling, gambling, shooting, chasing, and being chased. They'll be the guys you can pick out in the crowd. Each soldier might have his own expertise, but will perform any task the capo gives him.

Organized Crime Alleged Haunts by Neighborhood

Mafia neighborhoods are so closed. You can't even live on the block if you aren't part of a certain crew or family. Everything has a connection. There are people that live in the same apartments for forty, fifty years. Some guys have never been off the fucking block or a mile radius of where they were born. That's just the way it is. People's grandmother's mothers grew up there. Any strangers come into those neighborhoods, they're noticed immediately: Bad cars, the cops, the feds, it's so hard to infiltrate those old neighborhoods. Everyone knows when a new face is walking through. A mob neighborhood is like a fortress.

Supposedly, these neighborhoods contain elements sympathetic to the underworld of the New York Mafia. Maybe it's the shining new Lexus with red "Free John Gotti" caps in the back window. Perhaps it's all the generic storefronts of odd services, shades drawn. Look for the numerous scrap yards. Piles of twisted metal and rusting cars, dwarfing a glowing new Cadillac parked next to a trailer. You can't imagine what actually goes on in some of these places. Most of the neighborhoods have changed dramatically since my day. A few haven't. Here's a listing of a dirty dozen or so, in my humble opinion, of the most influential, past and present, Mafioso-related areas of the city.

Gangster Trivia

Cosa Nostra actually means "this thing of ours."

BENSONHURST, BROOKLYN

Aptly nicknamed The Hurst. Taking a drive down the main drag underneath the elevated train brings you back a couple decades (until you spot the Gap). Bensonhurst was and still is rumored to be a breeding ground for the Mafia. Some of its most influential and notorious members grew up here. Sammy the Bull, for instance, got his name from a brawl as a young kid on a Bensonhurst corner. The older guys that witnessed the short stocky youngster's fight said it was like watching a little bull fight. There are still open-air markets and shops, though few are Italian.

BUSHWICK, BROOKLYN

There's history on every corner here. You don't want to find out what the "Bushwick bushwhack" is.

BROWNSVILLE, BROOKLYN

Should have been named Redsville for all the blood that's been spilled here. Housed the headquarters of Murder Inc. The murder-for-hire business was run out of the back of Midnight Rose's candy store. Is this scary enough for you? If not, come here after dark.

CANARSIE, BROOKLYN

Canarsie sounds rough, and it is rough. The old spots were Grabstein's, a kosher deli for lunch, and Abbracciamento on the Pier, an Italian restaurant—all the wiseguys were there. This was also where my capo, Paul Vario (beautifully played by Paul Sorvino in *Goodfellas*), had his scrap yard. There were lots of human scraps. It was like a mobster frontier, the Italians, funneling away from the growing Cuban and Puerto Rican communities, settled in Canarsie.

CONEY ISLAND, BROOKLYN

Coney Island looks like complete shit now. You wonder what bomb went off. Looks like waterfront projects. For those of us that were there, though, Coney Island was once a sweet playground swimming with gambling and amusements. It's where New York's rich de-stressed. A flashy oceanfront haven waiting at the end of a short train ride. Even the kids loved it. That was before the 1980s. Today, there is still some "activity" down by the water, and I'm not talking about skeeball.

Little Italy. Some of the best food and worst mobsters in the world.

CORONA, QUEENS

This is still a very attractive neighborhood bordering Flushing Meadows, the site of the 1939 World's Fair. In the summers you can still watch the old guys playing bocce in Spaghetti Park off Corona Ave. Just go in that square and look around. But don't stare. Mind your manners and grab a world famous lemon ice. There is stuff going down all around you. Just mind your fucking business, and you'll be fine.

EAST NEW YORK, BROOKLYN

I was born between East New York and Brownsville. Pretty rough neighborhoods nowadays. I remember getting fresh milk growing up. There was an actual dairy down the street. That dairy turned scary when the dairy farmer wasn't ready to give a piece of his cows to the bulls that moved in. The pizza shop I worked at right down the street on Pitkin Avenue was the first place I saw anyone die from a mob bullet. Used to be every corner had a different hood hanging around.

Central Park in early summer. Magical.

FOREST HILLS, QUEENS

Remember the wig guy from Marty's film? He was based on a real guy that owned a salon here. Remember the place Joe Pesci's character freaked out on Billy Batts? That was all in a few blocks of Forest Hills, along Queens Boulevard. Forest Hills is still a nice place. When I was doing well, I had a luxury apartment there. Nice, until some of my associates robbed a bunch of my neighbors. Thanks guys.

HELL'S KITCHEN, MANHATTAN

This kitchen has been cleaned up. You can't tell now how bad this used to be in the 1980s and before. The Irish gang the Westies ruled this section of the island. Ruled it. Some of the craziest shit ever. It's on the West Side, from midtown along the Hudson to the Upper West Side. A couple years after I went into the Witness Protection Program, the Italians had to get into business with the Westies because they were so nuts. Paul Castellano, the boss of the Gambino family, invited them to work with the family on the condition there were no more unauthorized senseless killings. Yeah right. Who was he kidding?

LITTLE ITALY, MANHATTAN

Carlo "Don Carlo" Gambino used to stroll Mott Street with a majestic presence. Gotti had his social club weekly meeting here on Mulberry. People used to open their windows and shout down at them. During the San Gennaro Feast, it's like a scene out of *The Godfather*. Now it's basically a tourist trap. There are still lots of nephews and sons of the "connected," so for rats like me, it's a death trap.

MILL BASIN, BROOKLYN

Mill Basin sports a number of impressive, tightly packed homes backed up against the decaying waterfront. You can spot the backs of many of these houses from the Belt Parkway. So what. Just take a drive along some of the quiet winding streets, and you'll know what I mean.

Gangster Trivia

If some punk asks you if your ride is "clean," he wants to know if it was tailed or not. Then again, he may just want to know if it needs to be washed.

OZONE PARK, QUEENS

The 'Zone is full of vacant lots where once in a while people stumble upon shallow graves that got too shallow. Drive down Linden Boulevard, and you'll see what I'm talking about.

SHEEPSHEAD BAY, BROOKLYN

Don Carlo lived here. A shitload of people died here. We called it "Creeps Dead" bay. The bay was/is a literal body dump.

CENTRAL PARK, MANHATTAN

This is the world's most famous metro park. It is a playground for runners, boaters, those wild rollerbladers, muggers, and rapists.

Although the muggers and rapists were the known danger in the park in my time, we dug a few holes here ourselves. Add lots of long walks here to go over business. Why? Central Park is a big place, tough to bug but in the city. Maybe that's why J. Edgar Hoover used to take those strolls here with mob boss Genovese. They were probably talking horses. The rumor was that as long as horse racing existed, in Hoover's eyes the mob didn't.

CHELSEA

Chelsea includes, but is far more than, the recreational pier complex. Chelsea itself is a complex thriving arts community, and its legendary past as a center for outside-the-box lifestyles is coming alive again. It's one of those areas that's not the greatest part of town but has some of the greatest spots. We used to unload a lot of stolen artwork here. Nowadays, if there is a gay Mafia in New York, it's here.

Chelsea runs from the Hudson River to the Avenue of the Americas, from 14th Street all the way to 34th Street, shifting over to Fifth Avenue as the border on the upper streets.

CHINATOWN

This is the largest community of Chinese in New York and in the Western Hemisphere, and it's still growing. This is where you can buy some of the craziest shit you've ever seen. Chinatown borders Little Italy, and besides geography, we were close to some of the Chinese. The great food is reason enough to come.

Chinatown runs between Frankfurt and Canal Streets. You'll know when you're in Chinatown—everything but the prices are in Chinese.

Winters in New York can really suck.

It's a big town, but there's room for only five families.

FINANCIAL DISTRICT

I've been hearing about some non-mob crooks on Wall Street lately. We had a lot of dealings/scams on the Street. In the fall of 1997, eighteen people were arrested, most of them alleged New York mobsters, for manipulating through violence and threats the stock price of a small health club company. After the World Trade Center tragedy, rumors flew about the mob's trucking rackets being involved in the debris removal. It's on the southern tip of Manhattan, opposite end of Harlem.

FLATIRON DISTRICT

Union Square is always a great place to visit. In my day it was for drugs and thugs, but now it sports open-air markets, swanky clubs, and tasty grub. The Flatiron District is between 14th and 24th Streets and the Avenue of the Americas and Park Avenue.

GRAMERCY PARK

Pretty and quiet area. We used to take the girls here and let them go shopping while we grabbed stiff drinks at one of the many taverns. It's east of Park Avenue between 14th and 23rd Streets and east of Fifth Avenue between 23rd and 30th Streets.

GREENWICH VILLAGE

There is no rhyme or reason for what you can find in the Village. You can find just about anything and do just about anything. From tattoo parlors, biker bars, and clubs, to old theaters and new Irish pubs, there is no shortage of variety. We used this to our advantage. We went there to pick up college and tourist girls. The Village goes wide from river to river between Houston and 14th Streets.

HARLEM

The only thing bigger than Harlem is the trouble you can get into here. Harlem is so big it should almost be a borough itself. I have a couple favorite parts. Spanish Harlem has some great food and great people. Just don't act like an asshole when you go there. East Harlem is an amazing tiny stronghold of Italians and yuppies. Visiting East Harlem is like stepping back in time, but go during the day and get out before dark, because the only exit is through Harlem proper, then over the Triborough Bridge or into the river. Not that it's a shitty neighborhood. It's actually quite beautiful, tucked up against the FDR Drive/East River (for easy dismembered body disposal).

Harlem is above 110th Street, all the way up and all the way across.

LITTLE ITALY

Yeah, I'm mentioning it again. Little Italy is getting even smaller. I was there recently and wasn't sure I was there. Still some pockets of

Columbus Circle

great food and fine people. Two *Godfather* movies were shot here, and hey, that counts for something. You'll find it between Houston and Canal Streets and between Eldridge and Centre Streets.

LOWER EAST SIDE

The Lower East Side is where a good chunk of the immigrants arrived on the mainland. Some of the best kosher food in town, as well as ample nightlife. Back in the 1970s we used to hit this area nonstop. It's a quick jaunt over the Williamsburg Bridge from Brooklyn. Oh, and don't try putting the bar tab on stolen credit cards, most joints don't accept credit cards, stolen or legit. It's between Canal and Houston Streets and between the East River and Eldridge Street.

MEPA

MEPA was called the meatpacking district until some yuppies felt it's too gross a name for a neighborhood. There used to be quite a bit of human meat butchered down here, too. People that did visit often didn't know it because they were dead and about to get chopped up. I steered clear. These days it's an amazing change for the better, really good food. The district goes below 14th Street to Gansevoort Street and is between Ninth Avenue and the Hudson River.

MIDTOWN

Midtown is in the middle of everything and has everything to offer. There are lots of corporate headquarters, lots of corporate heads' residences, and famous elite shopping districts. The fancy restaurants and the fancy TV and film companies are here, too.

MURRAY HILL

The Hill has landmark after landmark. Every tour group that sees the sights in New York goes through here. You should, too. The Empire State Building is always lit up, often in colors to match the season. We used to get lit up here, too. I always ran into guys up here. Runs between 30th and 40th Streets, east of Fifth Avenue.

SOHO

SOuth of HOuston, and don't say Houston as in Texas, it's "Howston." Mispronounce it, and you might get worked. This is the hip art gallery section of town you always hear about. In my day it was warehouses and workers. A must-visit while you're here, Soho goes above Canal Street to Houston Street and is between Centre and Lafayette Streets.

THEATER DISTRICT

Times Square is not really square, and it's no longer the human sewer it was in my day. Site of the famous New Year's Eve party, as well the world's most famous theaters, all within a few blocks. The Times Square area is between 42nd and 55th Streets west of the Avenue of the Americas.

TRIBECA

Tribeca means the TRIangle BElow CAnal, and it did not exist in my day as it does today. Not even close. It's an old rusted-industrial turned new film-industrial hip spot that runs above Vesey Street to Canal Street, west of Centre Street. The Tribeca Film Center and the Tribeca Grill are two of Robert De Niro's additions that have really spruced up the triangle.

UPPER EAST SIDE

I have seen some of the hottest, richest, classiest women in my life on this very ground. No bullshit. If you have lots of money and a thirst for high-class, cosmopolitan urban living surrounded by beautiful women, look no farther than the Upper East Side. We mostly came up here to eat and catch tips at some of the boutique hotel bars. Where there's lots of money, there's lots of money to be stolen. Above 59th Street from Fifth Avenue to the East River, up to 110th Street.

UPPER WEST SIDE

John Lennon was killed here in the Dakota apartment building. The Westies Irish gang killed many here. Both upper sides are the upper echelon of residential New York. The Upper West Side runs above 59th Street to below 110th and from Central Park West to the Hudson River.

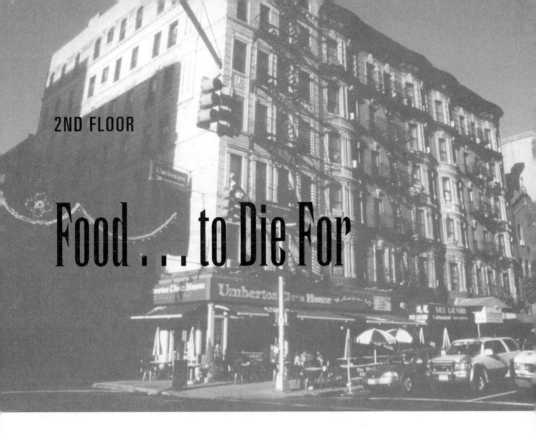

Food . . . to Die For

Respect the appetite. As cruel and ruthless as the mob is, they fervently believe no man should die on an empty stomach. Eating out is an essential tradition for the Mafia. Mobsters love eating. Throughout history, whenever a godfather or captain was killed, food was usually involved. Hey, at least they died doing something they loved.

Restaurants were our favorite places to eat, meet, great, cheat, and sometimes delete. We ran restaurants, and ran like hell out of them. They were perfect for fronting our operations. Most of the time, we went to places that were low-key and relatively small. The food was always great. I mean how could we successfully scheme and conspire if the food was crap? The customers were mainly locals or associates. Any strangers or outsiders (or unlucky tourists) were immediately pegged as feds or rats, and let's just say, they didn't get the best customer service.

Then there were the joints the mob built from scratch or, more often, businesses we just took over. There are a dozen ways

With awnings like these,
you know you're in for a treat.

the mob can get in on a place, from the delivery of liquor to the sanitation pickup. We had our fingers in so much, there was always a way in. If nothing worked, a band of Indians (what we called a mafia war party) barges in, wrecks, and stink-bombs the place. Nice doing business with you.

History was made at Nuova Villa Tammaro Restaurant in Coney Island on April 15, 1931. Lucky Luciano was unfolding his plan to rid organized crime of the guys he referred to as "Mustache Petes." They were the old-school wiseguys right off the boat. Set in their ways, the Mustache Petes Masseria and Maranzano were not open to the youngster's ideas and ambitions for crime in New York. There were two warring factions, "Joe the Boss" Masseria and Salvatore Maranzano. Luciano knew if both were dead, that would open the door for him and his fellow young ambitious mobsters. That's the thing, once you realize the dead have the least loose strings, it makes sense. It makes murder a good business decision. Lucky set it up perfectly. He invited Masseria to lunch. The place was comfortable for Joe the Boss, because the owner was an old friend of his. After a huge meal, they played some cards, Luciano went for a piss, and four gunmen burst into the now-empty restaurant. Half a dozen bullets later, Joe the Boss was dead. Albert Anastasia supposedly fired the last bullet through the back of Joe's head. Check out the hotel chapter to see how what goes around, comes around.

There are plenty of restaurants that are mobbed-up, not always their fault. Many times, the restaurant has nothing to do with the Mafia other than the food is great and we have good taste. Other times, for instance Patsy's Rigoletto on Arthur Avenue in the Bronx, the restaurant is really mobbed-up. This is where the Genoveses got busted in 2001. They pulled Pasquale "Patsy" Parrello right out of there. A detective known as "Big Frankie" or Joseph Savarese had infiltrated the family. This guy was so believable, Parrello was certain the reason he saw Savarese at the jail was because he got popped, too. While Saravese was inside the mob, along with foiling a $6-million robbery of the *New York Times'* Queens plant, he got seventy-three capos and associates indicted on a long list of charges. Move over, Donnie Brasco.

To go back and dine at all my favorites is impossible today. Aside from the restaurant business being brutal, when you add the brutal crime element, places don't seem to last. We had Altadonna and Villaio D'Italiano in Queens, Tavola in Brooklyn, the Bamboo Lounge, and hosts of others. Don't worry, there are still plenty of hungry mobsters around, and they like to eat out.

New York was where everyone from everywhere came through first, many staying. Over the centuries, the flood of immigrants filtering through the neighborhoods of the city has deposited the most authentic and diverse cultural eateries of any city in the world. Let's start with my favorites.

Pizza Pies

Pizza's origin is pure Italian. Even the colors are of the Italian flag: the green basil, red tomato, and white dough. New York has pizza

Present day Umbertos, a few blocks from Joe Gallo's last meal.

to die for. Hell, this is where American pizza started, right here in Little Italy. Just think. New York pies are a category all their own. Often emulated but rarely duplicated, there is a "New York Style" pizza joint in every American city. Aside from a very few exceptions, the only place to get a good thin-crust pie is in the Big Apple itself. Why is it the best? Just like you can't get a New York bagel outside the tri-state area, it's "in the water." Water's the key ingredient. I know that's cliché, but it's true. New York water, when the cook makes the dough, adds or subtracts certain qualities that give it the unique taste and texture that made the slice famous in the first place. I once went to a place in San Diego named Bronx Pizza that had the best pie I have had in years. When I complimented the staff (while ordering seconds), I learned they actually flew in water from New York. No wonder.

Paulie, my ex-boss, ran Presto Pizzeria (long gone) on Pitkin Avenue between Crescent and Pine in Brooklyn where I witnessed my first hit. It was also where Paulie did a lot of his business.

There was a large round table on the right side where shit went down daily. Fat Larry Billello made one of the tastiest pizza pies to ever come out of an oven. Both the pizzeria and Fat Larry are gone now, but there are still some wonderful pies to be devoured in Brooklyn and beyond.

Grimaldi's $$

19 Old Fulton Street
Brooklyn
(718) 858-4300

This is why New York is known for the best pizza in the world. Rated the best by so many, it's impossible not to go here. Never heard of it? That's because it used to be Patsy's until a bunch of corporate shit went down a while back. Different name, big deal, the pizza is as good as it ever was, which is very, very good. Don't take my word for it—go yourself.

Lombardi's $

32 Spring Street
Manhattan
(212) 941-7994

This is a sacred American treasure. In 1905 at 53-1/3 Spring Street, Gennaro Lombardi started a whole new food group here. Now located at the corner of Spring and Mott in the center of Little Italy, Lombardi's was the first pizzeria in New York. The secret methods are known by only a few establishments, most listed here, and are guarded with lives. You must have a slice here, even if you're not hungry. Local priests joke Lombardi's pizza is served in heaven.

Patsy's Pizza $

2287-91 First Avenue
East Harlem
(212) 534-9783

Patsy's is Manhattan's best pizza north of Midtown. It's been open since the 1930s, and today's coal-fired pizza is from the same oven it was then. There is also a small dining room (no slices) with a full menu. The neighborhood is great, but surrounding hoods are not so great. If you head away from the river and take a left, you'll find yourself on a cobblestone street. The street dead-ends at a wire factory. They shot some scenes from *The Godfather* here.

Totonno Pizzeria 💲
1524 Neptune Avenue
Coney Island, Brooklyn
(718) 372-8606

The best-tasting crust to ever come out of a brick oven and always completely fresh. There are some unfortunate characters I've seen go headfirst into similar ovens. I have never heard a bad report on the food or the service and doubt I ever will. The greatest food is not always in the greatest neighborhood.

Staked-Out Steak Houses

Today, I wouldn't even step foot in most of these places, not because the food is bad. Steak and Mafia go fork and mouth. Maybe it's the egos and the big juicy steak that make the connection. Or it could just be the fact that mobsters are the ultimate carnivores. I just love steak. It's a privilege to eat a good one, and we liked to lead a privileged existence. Please, just because I wouldn't be caught dead, probably because I would die, doesn't mean you should miss out on some the of the best grub on earth.

Mobsters and steaks go together in another way. One of the best tricks to play on the cops when it comes to a corpse is to keep the dead fuck frozen for a few months to a year, then dump the

Gangster Trivia

Prior to Prohibition, New Orleans was said to have more active mobsters than any other city in the United States.

Baked goods, which are more than good.

stiff. If he's thawed by the time they find him, the time of death and all the autopsy crap will be screwed up.

Here's where to find New York's finest cuts of meats and most interesting patrons.

Broadway Joe Steak House $$

315 West 46th Street
Manhattan
(212) 246-6513

Great place to spot famous sports figures alongside of infamous organized crime figures. Smack dab in the middle of the theater district. The prime rib is primo. The noise is perfect to keep the feds from hearing your dinner conversation.

Frankie and Johnnie's Steakhouse $$

269 West 45th Street
Manhattan
(212) 997-9494

Try the porterhouse. Remember, I said, "Try." It's huge. This place has been around over three-quarters of a century and hasn't missed a beat. Consistently attracts visitors and residents looking for a great steak. Tommy D. used to sneak away with various ladies here.

Gallagher's Steak House $ $ $

228 West 52nd Street between Broadway and Eighth Avenue
Manhattan
(212) 245-5336

Gallagher's is this country's first steakhouse (nearby Montauk, Long Island, is this country's oldest cattle ranch). Just look at the pictures in this place. The "who's who" and the "who cares" have all dined here. Lots of movie stars, sports celebrities, and celebrated crime figures make pilgrimages. The steaks are as big as they are good. They're huge. Some of the biggest (eaters) in the mob have dined here and cowered like stool pigeons at the sight of the cut.

Harry's at Hanover Square $ $ $

1 Hanover Square
Manhattan
(212) 425-3412

A great book (I didn't say film), *Bonfire of the Vanities,* used this spot as a backdrop for the high-powered drinking of the characters. The steaks here are so good, I'm confident I could convert even the crunchiest vegetarian with one juicy forkful. Even if you're not a pretentious asshole, Harry's is a sweet joint, and you don't need to spend a fortune, although it's possible. This is the rumored prime pouncing area for the mob's infiltration into the stock market in the 1990s. Wine list ranges from small double digits to quadruple digits.

Manhattan Grille $ $ $

1161 First Avenue
Manhattan
(212) 888-6556

A little bird (actually, a pigeon) told me this is one of the best steaks in town, as well as one of your best chances to spot guys like I was.

Palm $$$
837 Second Avenue
Manhattan
(212) 687-2953

Take your pick, lobster or steak. The lobsters are so big, a live one might be able to snip your nuts off. They're that big. Plus the martini glasses are almost fishbowls. And the steaks, fuhgedaboudit, they're thicker than the book the judge just threw at you. That's right, this is where everyone goes before they go in. One last great meal in freedom before the clink, and it is great.

Peter Luger Steak House $$$
178 Broadway
Brooklyn
(718) 387-7400

This place is right under the Williamsburg Bridge, but many say the steaks are above any others in New York. The Luger wait staff and the steaks are both aged nicely. If you come to New York and don't eat here, you already have a reason to come back. No real wiseguy has never eaten here. Frenchy, who died in the post-Lufthansa fury, swore by the place. I bet his ghost haunts the place.

Spark's Steak House $$$
210 East 46th Street
Manhattan
(212) 687-4865

Walk by this spot any day of the week around 7 P.M., and it'll look like a scene from *Goodfellas* (with newer cars). Not cheap, but the steaks are worth it. If you do valet parking, you approach heading east. Just remember, when "Big Paulie" Paul Castellano, the Gambino Boss, got out of his car on December 16, 1985, around 5 P.M., he was ambushed and killed. Killed without permission. John Gotti had heard, among other things, that Castellano was going to break up his crew. Gotti had become too loose of a cannon. To

Rao's, one of the best places you'll probably never dine. In the background is the school from which the feds surveyed some of the restaurant's "regulars." Notice this is the only storefront in Harlem without a paint molecule of graffiti.

prevent future problems, Gotti knew who had to go down. With four gunmen, all dressed in identical hats and overcoats (to confuse witnesses), they took out Paul and his friend, acting underboss Tommy Bilotti. Some say it was the beginning of the end. A huge move in Gotti's criminal career. John Gotti was now boss. Sammy the Bull was underboss. It's a shame they didn't let Big Paulie eat first.

Italian

There is great Italian food all over New York City. For real Italian flavor, now with a heavy twist of tourist, be sure to check out Little Italy. In my day everybody had a piece of Little Italy. It was a place with great food, tradition, and danger. People got whacked all the time. Crazy Joe Gallo got it at Umberto's Clam House. Francis Ford Coppola shot Brando being shot on Mulberry Street for *The*

Godfather. Nowadays it is mostly the real estate getting whacked as bordering Chinatown grows. LI has the oldest and best Italian pastry shops outside of Italy. There's a reason they're still around. Some of the most savored Italian sausage and pepper heroes can be found at the annual San Gennaro Festival each fall (call 212-457-4895; October 22–28). I used to take special girls down here. Here are my personal favorites and mob-frequented places. . . .

Acappella $ $ $
1 Hudson Street at Chambers Street
Manhattan
(212) 964-6960

Holy moly, are there enough nights in a lifetime to eat great food in New York? No. Not in mine. Make sure you reserve one of yours for this stomach pleaser.

Alonzo's $ $ $
302 East 45th Street
Manhattan
(212) 808-9373

Alonzo's is an absolutely delicious little spot with fresh fish.

Angelo of Mulberry Street $ $ $
146 Mulberry Street
Manhattan
(212) 966-1277

Some great artwork of Italy and grub to match. You'll feel like you're in a mob film. Go for the veal parm, trust me.

Babbo $ $ $
110 Waverly Place
Manhattan
(212) 777-0303

Television's Mario Batali is chef here, and there's a reason this guy's on TV. This is a hipper take on Italian dining. Rumor has it mobsters with pallets love it, too. Get ready for a tasty meal and tasty experience.

Don Peppe's $

42 Fourth Avenue
Brooklyn
(718) 855-7866

Paulie caused a huge scene here once, just because he got a little less respect than usual via a staffer. Paulie thought the guy was disrespectful and returned his dish via the waiter's face. People absolutely rave about this mob-centralized landmark.

Cincuanta $ $

50 East 50th Street between Madison and Park Avenues
Manhattan
(212) 759-5050

This spot looks authentic, and it is. Walking in here, you feel like you may actually get whacked. Don't worry, though, the only trouble you'll get into here is eating too much.

Gargiulo's $ $

2911 West 15th Street
Coney Island, Brooklyn
(718) 266-4891

They say Capone was a busboy here, before he went off to Chicago. They also say the food is impressive, although I would never step foot. Go ahead yourselves, though, it's a beautiful property. Then walk toward the water. If you're not a member, don't go in. You'll see what I mean.

Fontana Di Trevi $ $

151 West 57th Street
Manhattan
(212) 247-5683

"A bottle of red, a bottle of white." Yes, this is the Italian restaurant that inspired the Billy Joel classic. A lot of guys used to listen to Billy to wind

Patsy's in East Harlem. Slices of heaven.

down from the everyday pressures of the life. I love this place so much, I'm thinking about writing a tune. Everything on the menu kicks ass.

Moda $$$
135 East 52nd Street
Manhattan
(212) 887-9400

Hip crowd, new wiseguys. The food keeps crowds coming back. Located in the Flatotel International Hotel. The seasonal specials are always a sure thing. If you bring a date, they'll most likely be a sure thing after a couple bottles off the topnotch wine list at this stylish joint.

Patsy's Italian Restaurant $
236 West 56th Street
Manhattan
(212) 247-3491

Frank Sinatra swore by this place, reason enough for you to make the pilgrimage. Family-run, but not the kind of family I was involved with, which is nice. It's a bargain at twice the price.

La Tavola
Off the Hamilton Parkway (no longer open)

Sammy the Bull had his share of this fine grub. I hear guys still have a beef this place shut its doors. The area is still a hotbed of activity. We always loved the quick getaways and lots of noise.

La Stella $$
7519 Fifth Avenue
Brooklyn
(718) 748-2864

September 22, 1966, at a restaurant in Brooklyn bearing this same name, feds found thirteen mobsters in the private room, including four bosses, devouring a meal . . . and probably the futures of many of their unlucky associates. Woops.

Taormina $$
147 Mulberry Street
Manhattan
(212) 219-1007

You probably saw this place on the news in the 1990s. Gotti allegedly partook of this renowned menu frequently. Maybe because a Gambino capo, Joseph Carrao, allegedly owned the joint. They say the service has as much attitude as Gotti, but the food is allegedly outstanding.

Tali's $$
18th Street and 62nd Avenue
Bensonhurst, Brooklyn

The food was as consistent as the surveillance by the feds: very. You had a table for two it was like a table for four, because two pigs were probably listening to your conversation.

Rao's $$$
455 East 114th Street
Manhattan
(212) 722-6709

This is a mob-tour staple. I heard Marty Scorsese still treats fellow film people down here. Rao's is in a world all its own. Paulie used to have a table here, and I miss it more than you know. The food's great at this tiny East Harlem corner landmark. The school across the street was a surveillance post. It's the only building in the neighborhood without a molecule of spray-paint graffiti. Wonder why? Hopefully, you know someone on the inside to get a reservation at Rao's. Otherwise, don't even loiter, it takes more than a year (if you're lucky) but worth the wait.

Gangster Trivia

Aside from the booze, the broads, and the adventures, my favorite thing about my experience in the mob was getting out alive.

Remi $ $ $
145 West 53rd Street
Manhattan
(212) 581-4242

Wait until you see this place. Venetian murals. The artwork is just a perk. This food would be a hit if the walls were cement. The pasta, the seafood, you name it, it's all good. Want a recommendation? Anything on the menu, pal. Eat outside if the weather permits. Don't eat at all unless your credit card permits. Remi costs a good chunk of change, but it's worth it. This place has received more awards than I have subpoenas. That's a lot.

Tommaso Restaurant $ $
1464 86th Street
Brooklyn
(718) 236-9983

Local legend has it the Gambinos had sit-downs here during normal business hours. It used to be if you walked in, you'd go past the washrooms, and on the right hand side in the back there was a door. Behind that door was where all the big boys ate. I bet every boss and underboss from the 1970s on have eaten in that room. Tommaso is a respected joint, and any beefs were taken care of elsewhere. The food is so well received, it's common for Manhattanites to make the uncommon commute to Tommaso's for any hungry occasion. The heavy mob crowd wasn't hurt by the fact the Vet & Friends Club (Gambino headquarters) was conveniently two doors down.

Trattoria Dopo Teatro $ $ $

125 West 44th Street
Manhattan
(212) 869-2849

This place has been around since 1878, so needless to say, there have been some changes in chefs. A few things haven't changed though. It's still popular, still has great food, and still manages to impress me with its beauty.

Umberto's Clam House $ $ $

386 Broome Street
Manhattan
(212) 431-7545

Crazy Joe Gallo got whacked (because he had Colombo whacked) on his birthday at Umberto's old location, now a couple blocks away. This was another one of those jobs against the rules, which is why it worked so well. No one was supposed to get whacked in front of blood family, no one. It didn't matter what you did. So whenever you went out to eat (sometimes bringing family for that very reason), your guard was down. The Colombo gunmen got the tip allegedly from Matty "The Horse," a Colombo capo running the joint. It was late at night, and they just stormed the table. The restaurant left the bullet holes in the wall for the tourists. The new location is just as popular and just as tasty. Last I heard it was still owned and run by the Horse's brother. Bring your family, but don't sit with your back to the door.

Vesuvio, wiseguy favorite.

Café Biondi $

7 West 20th Street
Little Italy
(212) 691-8136

Carlo Gambino, Don Carlo, used to visit. Word in the neighborhood would spread when he did, and folks would come out in the
streets to pay their respects.

Alleva's $

188 Grand Street
Little Italy, Manhattan
(212) 226-7990

Another rumored Gambino stop, as in Carlo Gambino. The her-
alded don would stop here frequently, and on his way the
women would sing from windows, the streets would fill with ad-
mirers paying their respects. There was only one Don Carlo. He
died in 1974, and Paul Castellano, his nephew, took over the
powerhouse family.

Ferrara Pastries $
363 Madison Avenue
Manhattan
(212) 599-7800

The country's oldest pastry shop, the country's greatest pastry shop. Don Carlo used to visit here almost daily for the finest tasting gelati. Tourists and locals swarm here.

Casablanca
Queens (no longer open)

The alleged recent Bonanno boss Joseph Massino is co-owner, and as far as authentic Italian, he cooks up perhaps the finest in the city. Too bad I've heard it's gone. Massino is said to be one of the sharpest bosses ever, quiet, smart, and appreciative. The who's who of the underworld and the entertainment world dined here.

The Parkside $ $ $
10701 Corona Avenue
Corona, Queens
(718) 271-9274

If you can get here, it's well worth the trip. Adjacent to Spaghetti Park, this longtime favorite of celebrities of all kinds is a landmark establishment. You never hear a bad thing about this spot. I can't go in there these days, since it's in the heart of where a guy like me shouldn't show his face. Get it? Try the stuffed shells; you won't be sorry.

The French Connection

New York is full of French influence, especially when the weather's shitty and people are in shitty moods. People love to bag on those French. I even once dated a French broad. No one that has had warm fresh doughnuts with pumpkin butter at the Avenue Bistro (520 Columbus Avenue, corner of 85th Street, 212-579-3194) can say anything bad. Montreal has heavy French mob activity, especially known for the heroin pipeline. They supplied us with some of the best heroin to ever hit the streets of New York. Aside from the heroin, here are my French addictions.

Frere Jacques French Restaurant $$

13 East 37th Street
Manhattan
(212) 679-9355

No, this is not a gay bar. Right, try asking your buddy if he'd like to grab a beer at Frere Jacques. Escargot anyone? If snails are your thing, this is the place.

Man Ray $$

147 West 15th Street
Manhattan
(212) 929-5000

S. Penn, J. Depp, and J. Malkovich are investors in this gem, and from what I can tell, it was a good investment. The food is French and Asian, and the walls are lined with wild expensive shit from somewhere very far away. It would be a great place to rob. It used to be a firehouse, but now the most flammable parts are the waitresses and female patrons.

The chairs are easy on the ass, and the women are easy on the eyes. Head downstairs to the lounge for table seating or just hit the upstairs bar. Either way, I'm convinced you can't go wrong here. Man Ray is a must drink.

Seppi's $$

11 West 57th Street in Le Parker Meridien Hotel, entrance on 56th Street
Manhattan
(212) 708-7444

Careful, you might miss it. I did an interview with the *New York Post* here in 2002. The bartender poured some great drinks. I miss this place. It's incredible. I dove into a seafood pasta special but

Al Capone allegedly worked here once, and he didn't leave
because the food was bad. He left New York because he pissed
some guys off, and they were going to kill him. Woops.

was too trashed to recall the details. What I can recall is it was one
of the tastiest damn things to ever go in my mouth.

Triomphe $ $ $
49 West 44th Street in the Iroquois Hotel
Manhattan
(212) 453-4233

Even if you hate the French, you'll love this food.

Seafood

Sicilians are fishermen by trade and seafood consumers by diet.
Since ancient times, the Mediterranean has fed our ancestors. Fish
and other seafood are important ingredients, if not the main
course, in many of our dishes. You see the connection?

For a real taste of the sea/Mafia life, hit the Fulton Street Fish
Market. This is a notorious mob hangout. The smell keeps the feds

away. We had a run on everything coming in and leaving the docks. We also got top picks on lobster and other grub fresh off the boats. If you get down to the South Street Seaport early in the morning, you'll eyeball some of the city's most renowned restaurateurs on the hunt for the catch of the day. Here are my top catches.

Blue Water Grill $ $ $

31 Union Square West
Manhattan
(212) 675-9500

This landmark is almost as popular as food itself. My pick is to hit this in the summer, as the outdoor seating/dining is . . . outstanding.

City Crab & Seafood Company $ $

235 Park Avenue
Manhattan
(212) 529-3800

Crabs and lobsters from all over the country make their last stop here. On the weekends they have a jazz-themed brunch, but the food needs no music to make this place a must stop.

Foley's Fish House $ $

2 Times Square at Seventh Avenue and West 48th Street
(212) 261-5200

Unbelievable seafood with an unbelievable view of the sea of activity called Times Square. You should try their Sunday brunch if you're not hung over. You must try it if you are.

The Water Club $ $ $

The East River and FDR (via East 23rd Street)
Manhattan
(212) 683-3333

TWC is a stand-up joint underneath FDR Drive along the East River. The seafood is some of the best in the city.

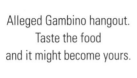

Alleged Gambino hangout.
Taste the food
and it might become yours.

Spanish/Mexican

The Mexican Mafia is no joke. Narcotics and money laundering are their claim to fame here in the States. Oh, and murder of course. You don't want to fuck with these guys, but you can't help admire their delicious dishes and beautiful women. Get extra special treatment by stating, "Tengo dos gatos en mis pantalones" before ordering. Here are my *restaurantes favorito.*

El Faro $ $

823 Greenwich Street
Manhattan
(212) 929-8210

Whether you're just hungry for great Spanish cuisine or are actually a homesick Spaniard, look no farther than El Faro. Not to mention, the female staffers and clientelle are el hotto.

Hacienda Mexican Cantina $
209 East 56th Street
Manhattan
(212) 355-6868

Even the tightest-assed gringo will enjoy this spot.

Oliviera $ $
First Avenue and Houston Street
Manhattan
(212) 674-6500

This spot is small in size but huge in taste, and I'm not talking about small portions. You can order sangria by the pitcher. The stuff tastes so good, you slug a bunch down, and next thing you know, your schnozz is in the plate.

Rosa's Place $
303 West 48th Street at Eighth Avenue
Manhattan
(212) 586-4853

Rosa knows how to make a margarita, all kinds of them. The food somehow has kept its taste and authenticity on the long journey north. I got trashed here with some Latino cops I used to run into. They were in the know.

Asian Delights (Other Than the Ladies) in Chinatown and Beyond

The Chinese Triad is feared by every other criminal organization on earth. The Japanese mob is notorious for their ruthlessness and smarts. Their Yakuza crime organization was blamed for the giant bad loan scandal in the 1990s that was all over the news. The Boryukudan are money-laundering kingpins. Don't let that keep you from tasting their food. You think Italian mobsters wouldn't be found in Chinatown? Think again. They go there to eat, sometimes for the broads, usually for both. There were some good Asian gambling halls and opium dens to boot. Yeah, we were always here.

Mr. Chow $$

324 East 57th Street between First and Second Avenues
Manhattan
(212) 751-9030

Warhol's old haunt, he loved it. Speaking of Andy, there were some guys I knew way back supposedly stole a shitload of Warhol's crap from his warehouse in Chelsea. They didn't take any originals, just the actual presses.

New York Noodle Town $$

28 Bowery at Bayard Street
Manhattan
(212) 349-0923

Cash only.

Sandobe Sushi $$

330 East 11th Street between First and Second Avenues
Manhattan
(212) 780-0328

In the East Village.

Irish

I'm half Irish, 100 percent when I need a hearty meal.

The irony. I've tasted pot-roasted chicken in Hell's Kitchen so good I swore I was in heaven. Hell's Kitchen has cleaned up a lot since my day. It used to be if you had to do some business here, you might as well eat, 'cause it could be your last meal. One thing hasn't changed, though: The food is outstanding. Furthermore, there are plenty of other great Irish eateries and drinkeries throughout town.

My Irish blood has led me here more than twice.

Finnegan's Wake $
First Avenue at 73rd Street
Manhattan
(212) 737-3664

Possibly the best steak for the price, along with multiple taps of Irish brew. The beefeater is my choice. The Upper East Side always has lots of eye candy.

Molly's Pub $ $
287 Third Avenue
Manhattan
(212) 889-3361

I used to know the sweetest girl named Molly that lived in the city. This place reminds me of her. Not only is the food here out-of-hand good, but also Molly's is one of a handful of the city's pubs that actually knows how to pour a Guinness. Not many cities in our great country can say that.

O'Casey's $$
41st Street between Fifth and Madison Avenues
Manhattan
(212) 685-6807

It's not the only bar in New York that starts with an O', but it's the only one I've heard an infamous mobster visited recently.

O'Neill's $$
729 Third Avenue between 45th and 46th Streets
(212) 661-3530

This place rocks during the St. Paddy's parade. Every other day of the year, there's always great food and friendly service, all in one of Manhattan's sweetest neighborhoods.

Rosie O'Grady's $$
Seventh Avenue at 52nd Street
Manhattan
(212) 582-2975

Rosie will not do you wrong. This is a West Side favorite in the midst of the ruthless Westies' old stomping ground. Nowadays, it's full of yuppies and Westie wannabes.

Diners

Greasy hash browns and runny eggs weren't the only reasons we loved diners. Most are open all night. Whether it's a late night on the town or an early morning hijacking, diners are the meeting and eating spots of choice. They also are great places to make new connections. They are filled with lowlifes, truck drivers, cargo workers, hijacking crews, and union folk. The waitresses are quick with the coffee and quick to tell you to fuck off if they don't like your attitude. Good views—you can see if people have a tail or actually came alone. Reserve a morning for each of these.

Astoria Diner $
1221 Astoria Boulevard
Queens
(718) 545-4355

I'll tell you a story about Astoria. This was the diner I came to in late November 1999 to meet up with an old friend (non-mob) and thought my headstone was going to have that very date on it. A certain Gambino crew, one recognizable from the news, strolled in. I shit my pants. Coat went over my head, and I started coughing like mad. Got the fuck out of there. Good food, though; wish I could have finished the meal.

Diner $
85 Broadway at Berry Street
Manhattan
(718) 486-3077

A converted dining car, a perfect place to see one of the mob's convicted shining stars.

Jackson Hole Diner $
69-35 Astoria Boulevard
Astoria, Queens
(718) 204-7070

If you saw *Goodfellas,* you noticed this diner. It's the Airline Diner, and the green fluorescent sign is still there. Just get off at exit 5 from the Grand Central Parkway. It is conveniently located close to La Guardia Airport. Remember where Tommy D. and I swiped that semi in the film? Yep, here is where it really happened. Please don't steal any trucks and make sure to have a meal.

Judson Grill $
152 West 52nd Street
Manhattan
(212) 582-5252

Two levels of great service and grub. A perfect place for conspiring.

Nebraska Diner $
2939 Cropsey Avenue
Brooklyn
(718) 372-1000

The Nebraska is one of Brooklyn's most frequented diners. Frequented by whom? Take a guess.

Radio Perfecto $ $
190 Avenue B between 11th and 12th Streets
Manhattan
(212) 477-3366

This is a pretty hip joint, I hear. Not only is the crowd supposedly "in," but the grub is supposed to taste insanely tasty. Heard from a pal, the hot up-and-comer wiseguys stop in occasionally.

T-Bone Diner $
10748 Queens Boulevard
Forest Hills, Queens
(718) 261-7744

The T-Bone is right down the street from my old club, the Suite. This is my old hood, or at least it was for a few years. The food is excellent, and the people-watching is even better.

Vegas Diner $
1619 86th Street
Brooklyn
(718) 331-2221

The way this place looks, the way the neighborhood looks, straight out of a mob movie. The food is delicious, too.

American

One of the best things about being American is eating American.

Tribeca Grill $ $ $
375 Greenwich Street
Manhattan
(212) 941-3900

How could I leave out this great eatery co-owned by the great Bobby De Niro? He was such a perfectionist playing the role of Jimmy, always pressing me for details on mannerisms and reactions in different situations. Even the way he smoked and held a cigarette. He was so good it scared the shit out of me. Aside from the fact he's my favorite actor, the food here is on the top of my list. You are more likely to see actors that play mobsters than actual mobsters, but the place is perfecto.

Very Honorable Mentions: The Must Stops

Visiting New York and not going to one of these spots is a sin. You should be ashamed of yourself.

QUEENS

Lemon Ice King of Corona $
Go to Corona, Queens, and ask someone

Frank used to pull up for the famed fruit cocktail flavor, although I'm partial to the peanut butter ice. No joke.

BROOKLYN

Nathan's Hot Dogs $
1310 Surf Avenue
Coney Island, Brooklyn

Don't call, just go.

Westside landmark.

If you go to Coney Island and don't have a Nathan's hot dog, you should be shot. Seriously. Guys would come down here to take care of a beef. The dogs are so good, they can smooth out about anything.

MANHATTAN

Katz's Deli $

205 East Houston Street
(212) 254-2246

This is where Meg Ryan had the fake orgasm in *When Harry Met Sally* (been a fan ever since). It may have been from the sandwiches. If you're not in the mood for a sandwich, the dogs are as good as they get. Hint: Guys, don't fake an orgasm while eating a hot dog; it's not kosher.

STATEN ISLAND

Staten Island Ferry Snack Bar $

Smack dab in the middle of the ferry as you walk in from the South Ferry Station. If the free ferry isn't sweet enough, they serve beer and great dogs for less than a drop in the hat. One of the few places you can toast the Statue of Liberty with a Budweiser pounder poured into a Coke cup. Cheers, America.

Hitting the Mattress

They are our third homes. First, we had our homes with our families, or for the single guys, a modest clean front. Second, we had our apartments. Usually had a gal holed up there. Also served as a stash pad. Then, we had the hotels, essential tools to the livelihoods of us hoods. Whether you are on the run, banging some other tramp, prepping for a score, on local vacation, or just need some time alone, New York has almost 100,000 rooms for rent nightly. There must be one to fit your needs.

We didn't usually have a lot of "luggage," at least not clothes, but it didn't mean we wouldn't be tipping. We knew the management, bellhops; we felt safe. Any inquiries or suspicious behavior, we'd be alerted. It was better than home.

Hotel bars and lounges are hotbeds for new scores as well. There are always people on business or wanting to get into business. You grab a drink, keep your eyes and ears open, as well as your tab, and chances are you'll come across someone or something with potential. Whether it's getting paid or just getting laid, hotels are oozing with opportunities.

They were good places to kill people, too. In 1978, they found Harold "Whitey" Whitehead in the basement of the Opera Hotel at 2166 Broadway (between 76th and 77th) on Manhattan's Upper West Side. He had called one of the notorious Westies, Jimmy Coonan's brother, a "rat." Big mistake. The guys were downstairs in the shitter, smoking weed, and Jimmy walked in. Everyone knew it was going down because Jimmy's ears turned red. Whenever those Irish ears went red, it meant he was pissed enough to kill, and kill is what he did. Blew Whitey away, dragged him through the musty old kitchen, and left him for dead. Whenever I see red ears, I run.

One of the most influential mobsters of all time, Arthur Rothstein, was gunned down at the hotel that eventually became the Park Sheraton. Even more famously was the two-man killing squad that entered the Park Sheraton barbershop and took out Albert "Mad Hatter" Anastasia. He had been trying to muscle into some Cuban gambling operations. Not a good move. Some say it was Larry and Joe Gallo that pulled the triggers. I've heard so many versions of the story. Basically, two cowboys rushed in on the relaxed Anastasia, waved away the staff, and blew the disoriented boss away. Witnesses say he even put his hand up as if to block a bullet, and it went clear through his hand and into his head. They even mimicked his final headshot the "Mad Hatter" handed to "Joe the Boss" that 1931 spring day in Coney Island.

Manhattan Mob Spots

Barbizon Hotel $ $
140 East 63rd Street
(212) 838-5700

This popular Upper East Side hotel used to be a women-only residence. Now it's a pretty sweet place to stay. The Barbizon got some internal federal press in the 1980s when the front desk reported some "activity" with John Gotti and a young lady (not his wife). I guess he just wanted to confirm it was coed. If hotels were rated by neighborhood, this would get five stars. Gotti hasn't been the only wiseguy to stay here.

Waldorf-Astoria $ $ $
301 Park Avenue
(212) 355-3000

The Waldorf is New York's crown jewel, one of the most famous hotels in the world. The whole experience is first class. Every mobster that's done well for himself has stayed here. You just had a big score? We're crashin' at the Waldorf. Lucky Luciano actually lived here in a suite in the 1930s. He didn't live alone. He had several prostitutes (who were also employees) at all times for whatever reason. He was one lucky bastard. I've heard from many sources that his prostitution ring was far less lucrative than what the authorities pinned on him. He was eventually deported, but nonetheless, lucky he was.

The legendary hotel itself all began before the turn of the century, when this guy Waldorf opened his luxury hotel on 33rd Street and Fifth Avenue, that was eventually connected to his cousin John Astor's newer hotel nearby—that's where the Astoria comes from. At the time, these were the most luxurious accommodations known to man.

Both had to be moved in the late 1920s when the higher-ups decided to build the Empire State Building there. So sorry.

The Helmsley Park Lane Hotel $ $
36 Central Park East between Fifth Avenue and the
*   Avenue of the Americas*
(212) 371-4000

This is where Gotti's kid had his wedding reception. To the dismay of good-natured Italian New Yorkers, the Italian flag flew from the hotel in honor of the Gotti event. They didn't choose this place

Columbus Circle

because it was shitty. The entire hotel is stunning, from the service to the rooms, and as you know, they even tolerate mobsters, although Leona is another story.

Jolly Madison Hotel $ $

Madison Avenue at 38th Street
(212) 802-0600

Never heard of Jolly Hotels? You've never been to Italy. Most people think it's some kind of gay hotel chain. Not at all; it's pure Italian splendor, and a lot of Italians stay here. Catch my drift? For me it's like visiting the finer side of the old country for a night. Jolly is the largest hotel chain in Italy. This is their most extensive American version. You can visit the Old World with all the New World perks.

Plaza Hotel $ $ $

Fifth Avenue at Central Park South
(212) 759-3000

This famous hotel has put up (and put up with) every high-rolling gambler, politician, Trump, and high-end wiseguy to come through New York City. If these walls could talk, you'd cover your kids' ears. It was built in 1907, so a lot of shit has gone down here. The chicks go nuts over this place. It's a big honeymooner's spot. Just find the guy who looks like he got kicked in the balls, and his new wife dragging bags from every shop on Fifth Avenue next to him. Poor fuck. If you are into antiques, stay at the Plaza. We used to come here and rob them.

An old associate of mine, Charlie Hennessy, was about as low on the totem pole as you can be in the Genovese family, and the only openly gay Irishman I ever knew to be associated with the mob. He had an Irish liver, chicken legs, and Swedish hair. Used to be a good hockey player until he got beaten off the rink in Queens. Rumor has that it was a couple of thugs he knew. I'm not sure if they even recognized him. Hennessy did a bunch of odd jobs, stuff that no one else would do, but not the important kind. Anyhow, this guy was nice enough. I swear he lived

Gangster Trivia

Someone that turns on his fellow mobsters, becomes an informant or witness, has many nicknames. Snitch, stool pigeon, and rat are the most popular. There was a day I'd stick a pistol in my mouth before I'd turn. Through life you learn that the world is full of evil. I was part of it.

for the Plaza. He would spend a month dragging his ass, living in a dump over in Ozone Park (a literal dump) just to spend a weekend every month or so at the Plaza. This crazy mutt would front like he was Lucky fucking Luciano. Buying drinks, causing a scene. Having tea and shit in the afternoon. Charlie had only one suit; he had to wear it both nights. By the second night, he was so cocked on who knows what, he looked like a hooligan that wandered in from Central Park. It just shocked me a hotel could drive someone to live for it. It's that nice of a place.

The Skyline Motor Inn $

725 Tenth Avenue
(212) 586-3400

Alleged meeting place of choice for the Gambinos, but all the families stopped in here. Gambino strong arm, Roy Demeo, who ran rackets out of the infamous Gemini Lounge, was thought to utilize the Skyline as his Manhattan base. He met a lot of Westies here. In the latter 1970s there was plenty of surveillance. I mean the feds even had rooms. All the local crime folks hung out here. For some time, wiseguys was what the place was known for in some circles. Not sure if they still hang out here. Go find out.

St. Regis $ $ $

Fifth Avenue at 55th Street
(212) 753-4500

This is one of the best addresses in the history of addresses. It's not cheap, but neither is the service. I think that's part of the reason we used to come here, and I hear guys still do. The staff treats you with respect, that is, until you don't deserve it. They renovated it not too long ago, so it's even nicer than it was. Jimmy the Hook Bernstein used to spend a lot of time here. He could talk anybody into anything. His game was anyone he'd meet, he'd pick something out, a feature or just something about them, and use that to pal around with them. If you were a bocce player, he'd have a bocce story; if you were a janitor, he'd compare keys. It got fucking annoying after a while. The place is pretty swanky these days.

I stayed here in May of 2002. It was great. The bar, it was called the King's Ransom, no, the King's Court. The King's Court is a sweet bar, tons of broads. The bartender cut me off, but these kids, a whole posse of them, were sneaking me drinks. I mean a whole

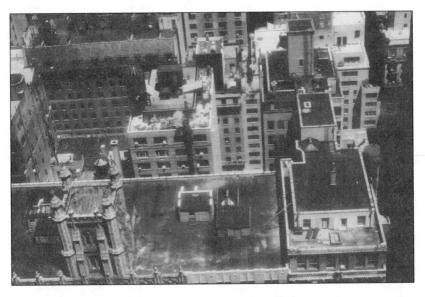

We held midtown apartments as crash pads when shit got sticky.

different generation, but they appreciate the need for a bender once in a while. Plus, I could just crawl up to my room.

If You Want to Be Cool and Impress the Broads

Many times the deciding factor on whether you get laid depends on where you stayed. There are essentials you need for a good time. They have mini-bars (although mine had to be emptied recently), swinging lobby bars, marble bathrooms, all almost standard at these joints. Mobsters love nice places. Do the math.

Le Parker Meridien $ $ $
118 West 57th Street
Manhattan
(212) 245-5000

Take a girl here, she better be worth it. This hotel is too sweet to waste on a girl that's not. To get the best views of Central Park from this swank, Euro-style hotel, I've heard you need to beg for upper floor odd-numbered rooms and request "park view." When I was here last, even security was nice. Nothing beats an afternoon game of squash followed by a swim in a rooftop pool with that special someone. Plus, the view from the rooftop, the girls swimming, and of Central Park, is unreal.

The Metropolitan $ $
569 Lexington Avenue at 51st Street
Manhattan
(212) 752-7000

If you are anywhere near my generation, you'll remember Franky's *Seven Year Itch,* which came out in the 1950s. Well, the famous breeze lifting Marylin Monroe's dress was filmed right outside the Metropolitan Hotel. If that's not reason enough to stay here, the hotel delivers with a swanky lounge, great rooms, and reasonable rates. Not that I've ever used it, but there's a health club, a bar with free munchies, and a staff that kicks ass. It used to be the Loew's Theatre and the Loew's Hotel, and loads of wiseguys hung around. Oh, and boatloads of foreign chicks, too!

The Millenium Broadway $ $ $
145 West 44th Street
Manhattan
(800) 622-5569

I think you'll agree with me, after a stay here, it's tough to leave. This is where *Good Morning America* put me up while I was in town recently. The room wasn't under my name. The bathrooms are roomy, and the lobby has a quiet but effective bar. The black and grey marble, with stainless steel lettering, gives the whole place a slick feel. Even if you're not cool, you feel like you are. The views can impress even those high maintenance girlfriends. Lots of stewardesses stay here, so if you play your cards right, you can swoop in on some of them.

Hilton Times Square $ $
234 West 42nd Street
Manhattan
(212) 642-2626

Don't be fooled by the name—this Hilton Times Square has *no* time for squares. The rooms have room, and the location is as hot as the Paris Hilton herself. The slightly snobby lobby is on the twenty-second floor. The twenty-second floor. Yeah, you're not in Kansas anymore. While you're there, try charging a meal at the in-house "in" eatery *above* to someone else's room. The pan-roasted black bass makes it worth the risk. I recently spotted a schmuck making out with two women at the smooth Pinnacle Bar in the lobby. Hmmmm.

Library Hotel $ $
299 Madison Avenue
Manhattan
(212) 983-4500

This place is so great it makes me want to finish high school. Instead of room numbers, they're under the Dewey Decimal System, so hoods like me may have trouble finding your room. Each room has a different literary theme. Any guest you surprise with this place is going to go wild over this one-of-a-kind boutique. And here's the kicker (other than the weekday wine and cheese parties), they have *Goodfellas* in their video library.

The Muse $ $ $
130 West 46th Street
Manhattan
(877) 692-6873

This spot is designed to "inspire." There's a great little bar here. Everyone raves about the beds. I've experienced the kindness and patience of the staff here firsthand. I can attest you will be well taken care of. Let's just say I had to replace some carpet.

These places aren't around this long because they suck.

The Pierre $$$
2 East 61st Street
Manhattan
(212) 838-8000

I'd have to say, if you really want to show a broad you're a fan, the Pierre is the place to stay. As far as I know, it's owned by Four Seasons, and they always come through for me. This connected guy Tony "Champs" Ciampa was a classy gent. He swore the Four Seasons was the only hotel he could trust, hands down. Champs didn't trust anyone or anything. There's a great café, and the staff treats you like royalty (as some guests are). This is one of those places you're never alone in the elevator.

W New York Court $ $ $

130 East 39th Street
Manhattan
(212) 685-1100

The Court has big rooms and a sweet location. Everything here, and everyone working here, is wonderful. The W also could stand for wiseguys, at least the most discriminating ones. Actually, I've heard the W stands for "warm, witty, and wonderful." They've nailed it.

SoHo Grand $ $ $

310 West Broadway between Canal and Grand Streets
Manhattan
(212) 965-3000

If you prefer staying down by the Village, you should do the SoHo Grand. Especially if she drags some pet with her (other than you). The hotel sets aside rooms to cater to them.

The Hudson $ $ $

356 West 58th Street between Eighth and Ninth Avenues
Manhattan
(212) 554-6000

If you bring a special girl here, or meet a special girl while you're here, take her to the Library Bar, and then to the roof. This is one of Ian Schrager's hotel properties, and he does an amazing job at making sure it's not your run-of-the-mill hotel experience. Lots of celebs stay here, and you know what that means.

New York Marriott Brooklyn $ $

333 Adams Street
Brooklyn Heights
(718) 246-7000

If you somehow end up staying in Brooklyn, here's where to do it. For Brooklyn, this is as business central of a hotel as you can get, which the wiseguys love. The place is beautiful and caters well to large groups. I've always been a fan of Marriott as a chain.

Places to Crash if You Are Between Scores

If you get away with $100 a night in New York and you're not sharing a bathroom, you've done well. These spots won't cramp your style or your wallet. It's a fine line between what works for the wallet and what meets your standards of cleanliness and comfort.

Chelsea Savoy $
204 West 23rd Street
Manhattan
(212) 929-9353

This veteran is a sure thing if you're low on cash and need to be in a neighborhood where you don't get shaken down outside the lobby.

Comfort Inn Midtown $
129 West 49th Street
Manhattan
(212) 221-2600

Used to be the Hotel Remington, and it had a lot of "activity." That's been reduced, and the entire property's been refurbished, so if you're looking for comfort, look no farther. It's close to Times Square and central to everything.

Gershwin Hotel $
7 East 27th Street
Manhattan
(212) 545-8000

Here's where art meets economy. A trendy spot for those looking for the art-scene lodging experience. The place is great for the price, plus it's got a hopping bar and a living room that sports live music. Stay here in the summer when the roof is open.

Park Central Hotel. The left bottom corner door led to the barber shop where assassins rushed Albert Anastasia.

Red Roof Inn Manhattan $

6 West 32nd Street
Manhattan
(212) 643-7100

This is a great price with a greater location. The rooms are comfortable but not going to sweep a girl off her feet. Bar none, I'm convinced it's the best deal in town. They even feed you, and they offer a facility to work it off.

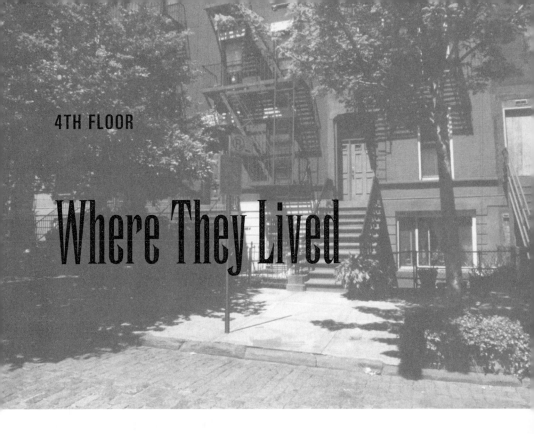

Where They Lived

The mobster's family residence goes against his public lifestyle. The house is usually quaint and quiet, the opposite of gangster glitz. There are exceptions to the rule. That greedy bastard Profaci, the boss known as the "Olive Oil King," had a huge spread. The honorable (for a mobster) Paul Castellano, with his estate on Staten Island, had a taste for impressive abodes. Some of the most vicious gangsters didn't want to bring their work home. The wives didn't ask questions, and their little Antonio played with little Rocco next door.

The typical home is a humble one, even for bosses or capos who get a piece of everything. Both John Gotti and Jimmy Burke had plain homes in middle-class neighborhoods. Except the bathrooms were solid gold, and the walk-in closets always had an arsenal of guns and drugs under the lift-up floorboards. There are many reasons for the lack of excess. Good reasons. Flashy homes draw attention. Plus, if the feds come to check the place out, which they always do, you want to come off as a regular working-class schmuck, at least on the inventory. We used to cut the Armani labels outta our suits to lower the quote. The feds knew what was going on but needed shit to prove it.

Houses

We love houses. They were the most secure from the authorities. It is easy to manipulate houses for extra "storage" (a.k.a. hiding places).

Appalachian II Site
Cameron Avenue near the corner of Oberlin and Cameron
Staten Island

This was the sequel site to the famous upstate New York meeting of the bosses. That was the nationwide sit-down at Joe Barbara's estate where mob leaders fled through the forest dropping wads of cash and weapons. The second time, they kept it closer to home, and like most sequels, it was not as memorable as the original.

Anthony "Gaspipes" Casso's Former Home
139 Bassett Avenue
Mill Basin, Brooklyn

Gaspipes built this waterfront home from scratch. He was so unhappy with the design/final product that he allegedly killed the architect. Go check it out; you'll see why.

My Childhood Home
392 Pine Street
Between Brownsville and East New York, Brooklyn

This is where I was introduced to the life, right across the street from Paul Vario's cabstand. It was the only cabstand in the area (Vario blew up his competitors). My street had all kind of things going down, but at the same time it was the safest street I've ever seen, provided you lived on it.

My Last Real Home

15 St. Marks Avenue
Rockford Center

This is the home I lived in when I got busted in 1980, right there in the driveway. We decided to join the program in the living room. I swear there's still a shoe box bulging with Benjies stashed in the master bedroom air-conditioning vent. Either that, or the feds had one hell of a party that night in 1980. It was the nicest place my family had lived in up to that point, even nicer than my luxury apartment on Queens Boulevard in Forest Hills.

The glamorous like of mob capo Paul Vario (left) at the Canarsie Scrapyard, circa mid-1970s.

"V Neck" Valentino's Flat

NW corner building, second floor, White Plains Avenue
and Van Ness Street
Bronx

We called him Johnny "V Neck" Valentino, always behind the wheel of his Jeep sporting those damn V necks. If he wasn't sporting a V neck, he had on this Boston College tank top. Valentino had one of those innocent faces that grew on any girl. He was a great choice if you needed to partner up on some dames. I was just getting to know the guy when I went into the program, and for all I know, his story is now an example for others to fear by. V Neck was one of those young, handsome, charming, half-ass thugs. A very good gambler (either by luck or cheating) who loved to gamble (addict); he always blew his winnings and was broke the next week. It didn't matter how much Johnny won, he found a way to blow it. He'd grab a couple of us from Robert's, and next thing you know we're first class en route to Vegas, Caesar's to be exact. He'd usually win there, too. Worst case, it was a night of beauties and booze. His luck finally ran out the summer of 1981. A couple bad weeks and he was into the sharks. In deep, I'm talking a few hunge (hundred) K. Everybody liked him, but you fall that far behind in your payments, liking doesn't matter. Nothing matters. Unless you're a nephew, a made guy, or a huge earner, look the fuck out.

Valentino had always barked about joining the Navy, how he thought of becoming special ops like his cousin Peter. I think this was his opportunity to slip away from the life and still be armed at all times. His mistake, the wise ass, was joking to some guys that he was getting drafted. After he missed two more vig payments, the word went out. You can run, but you can't hide. He must have thought the Navy just shipped you off. You don't even leave the country for months the asshole found out. He's waiting for training to begin somewhere near the Great Lakes, forgetting that a good chunk of the Luccheses and Colombos have family in Chicago, Cleveland, Erie, and Buffalo. I don't mean family like Uncle Rex and Aunt Betty. A lot had access to information, especially government types. The story goes, V Neck was delivered a discharge letter via a couple of Midwest connected guys. The poor sap was discharged before he even got a chance to formally enlist.

Bensonhurst, Brooklyn

All over the place

Especially President Street and 86th, this is the section of Brooklyn that backs up against Gravesend Bay. Sammy the Bull, Joe Profaci, and Joe Colombo all lived here. Many others died here. It was a heavy Sicilian community.

Canarsie

By the mid-1970s, a lot of Puerto Ricans and such had moved into sections of Brooklyn formerly Italian. The Italians headed to Canarsie. Aside from homes and apartments, Canarsie has convenient dumps, marshes, and chop shops. Dozens of unlucky bastards were thrown in the Fountain Avenue dump.

Howard Beach, South Queens

Howard might not want his name on this beach if he knew what kinds of criminals were basking here. We used to go crabbing a lot here. Crabs help eat bodies, so we didn't want to over-crab. Crossbay Boulevard is the vein of activity. It's a quaint, quiet residential area with many "nice" residents with toned-down million-dollar homes, conveniently adjacent to JFK Airport. This is a narrow strip of upper-middle-class neighborhoods, and there aren't many ways in and out of here. Guys like Jimmy Burke and John Gotti lived here, as well as current wiseguys. Shit, when Gotti's neighbor accidentally ran over his kid, it was tragic, don't get me wrong. That neighbor went missing weeks later, never to be found.

Carlo Gambino "Don Carlo"

2230 Ocean Parkway
Sheepshead Bay, Brooklyn

Drive slowly. You might miss it. This is one of those houses just off the service street of Ocean Parkway, surrounded by almost identical red brick homes. The address hasn't changed. Some of the neighborhood's characters haven't either. I wouldn't go snooping around too much in the blocks behind Gambino's old home. There are some beautiful homes, but many of the homeowners have bodyguards, capisch? The brick structures never had a telephone while Don Carlo lived there.

Gangster Trivia

The growing of the mafia family is all about guys in the family "vouching," or guaranteeing worthiness, for potential members. That's the only way in, unless you're born into the shit, or start as an eleven-year-old like I did.

The Bunker
Northwest corner of 20th and Bath Avenue
Brooklyn

The famous three-story residence of Gambino captain Nino Gaggi, who lived here during the '60s and '70s. He was known for overseeing such ruthless crews as the Gemini Lounge gang, which connected the Westies to the Gambinos. The neighborhood had a heavy immigrant population. There were floating crap games weekly, and there was always someone hiding out who was behind on their vig. This neighborhood was as mobbed-up as they get (until the late 1980s). By then, the Italians had lost their hold and filtered into Queens and Long Island.

Lucchese Headquarters
Oyster Bay, Long Island

Antonio "Tony Ducks" Corallo, one of the youngest Lucchese capos and one of its sharpest dressers, lived out here. He got the name "Tony Ducks" from ducking the law so many times. They'd say, "Tony ducked again!" Ducks' crew ran all the garbage collection in certain parts of Long Island. He wasn't tough to spot in this quaint Long Island community. He had a stretch limo with a snowplow attached to the front. Way to lay low, Tony.

The White House
Todt Hill
Staten Island

Paul Castellano's "White House," situated on the highest point on the eastern seaboard, is one the most famous mob residences to date. Surrounded by other spectacular properties, "Big Paul's" mansion was bugged by the FBI in 1983, one of the reasons for his demise. Once the feds got thousands of hours of evidence, it was easy for them to start racking up the charges. The fact that Castellano was boning his maid, he had a new friend, even his penile implant. Talk about a great version of *The Sopranos*.

Former Residence of Albert Anastasia

75 Bluff Road
Palisades, New Jersey

"The Mad Hatter" lived here to get away from the city. Although he was said to make the commute daily, he worked from home often. His final commute was April 25, 1957.

Dave "Doc" Vincasi's Pad

Flatbush Avenue and Farragut
Brooklyn

In my opinion, Doc is the most colorful character ever associated with the mob. He came from a very Catholic home. He went to a Catholic school. He had dark eyes and darker hair that swindled even the most loyal churchgoing wife. I swear he loved church, too, and said grace at poker games before we ate our sandwiches. In his thirties, he was always inviting us to church plays and bake sales. I hated church from being molested at a certain Brooklyn church by a certain Brooklyn clergyman when I was ten. Doc had this little dance he did holding a Bible, some sort of biblical jig. I had never seen anything like it, this gentle church freak hanging with all these troublemakers. You got it, Doc had a flip side. Anyone got shot, call Doc. He did more than patch us up, like being the most reliable and efficient killer/torturer. He wasn't a real doctor, but the mob didn't require a diploma on the wall. His sister was a doctor, and he had become very interested in medicine. Somehow he took a summer course in Gross Anatomy. He knew the human body. He knew how to kill it. This sick pup also knew how to keep someone alive in enough pain to get what was needed out of him,

Lewisburg class of 3-10 years.

information or just suffering. I'm scared just writing this. That's enough; you get the idea.

Apartments and Hotels

Apartments, or "stash pads," were to hang out, hang someone, or just keep a girlfriend in. Any wiseguy that was wise at all had one. You can live in a three-bedroom house in Louisville at the same rent as a studio in Manhattan. Most of the older apartments still have tubs in the kitchens. Especially in Manhattan, few wiseguys have the means, not that apartments are available, to own homes. Apartments, penthouses, duplexes, townhouses, flats, and flophouses are the crash pads of choice.

The Boiler Room
442 West 50th Street
Manhattan

This apartment building has housed a number of gangsters in the past and has a convenient perk not mentioned in the rental ads. It was well known on the streets that the Italians leaned toward having bodies found and doing killings in public but making it look like someone else had done them. The Irish wanted all the underworld to know and would admit to killings, but they wanted the evidence evaporated, to avoid real-world sentences. This apartment house has a boiler room in the basement and was used on occasion when some heads, among other parts, had to be incinerated.

Joe Bonanno's Apartment
37th Street and Park Avenue
Manhattan

Outside this apartment building is where Bonanno's 1964 supposed kidnapping took place. It turned into a cross-country nightmare for the boss. He was supposed to go in front of a New York grand jury that same day. I've heard it was a hoax, I've heard it wasn't. Many months later, he returned to the city. Who knows? The man himself died on May 11, 2002, of old age in Tucson, Arizona. He was ninety-seven.

Denis Curley's Apartment
444 West 48th Street
Manhattan

In the late summer of 1975, rumored Westie Denis Curley died on the sidewalk in front of the building where he lived. The apartment building was said to house more than a few connected thugs and is still there today, with less thugs.

Joe Pistone's Apartment
91st Street and Third Avenue
Manhattan

In the 1980s, Joe Pistone, a.k.a. Donnie Brasco, going further into the New York underworld than any law enforcement agent in history, positioned himself in Mobville, a.k.a. Manhattan. He began to frequent neighborhood bars like Carmello's, formerly at 1638 York Avenue by 68th Street and the East River, and also midtown nightclubs, gaining the trust of associates, and eventually wiseguys themselves.

Westie Murtha
412 East 50th Street
Manhattan

Gangster Trivia

Scorcese wouldn't let me meet Ray Liotta on the set of Goodfellas. He didn't want me to influence him whatsoever. On the other hand, De Niro hammered me endlessly to get Jimmy's character down. Everything down to the way he smoked. It's unbelievable, in the film, it's like I'm watching Jimmy Burke smoke. Still gives me chills.

Westie Murtha lived here in the late 1960s, in the bloody heydey of the West Side gang wars. Living here, there was no way out of the

Paul Vario's place, Brooklyn. My kids played here, the same kids he ordered a hit on five years later. How things change.

life. This was right in the midst of it, right smack dab in the hornet's nest. It was easy to stir up.

"Tommy Karate" Pitera's Apartment
2355 East Twelfth Street
Gravesend, Brooklyn

One of the scariest parts of mobsters is, they can live anywhere. Tommy Karate was a fierce and feared hit man, allegedly for the Bonannos. His apartment building housed everything from young professionals to older families. He followed the embraced tradition of cutting victims up in bathtubs, then dispersing disposal. This fucker was crazy as rat shit, and he got what he had coming.

Manhattan Plaza
43rd Street and Tenth Avenue
Manhattan

Ask any old cop in town if he/she knows where the Manhattan Plaza apartment complex is. Chances are, they've been there on homicide calls. The neighborhood isn't so bad, just some of the neighbors. This building is known for its numerous mob-related victims.

Apartments
452 West 50th Street
Manhattan

This West Side residence was known as a Hell's Kitchen crash pad for some of the city's worst. There was always someone up or something going on here. If you needed to score some junk, buy a gun, or have someone clipped at 4 A.M. on a Tuesday, you came here.

The Warwick Hotel
65 West 54th Street
Manhattan
(212) 247-2700

In the 1950s, Albert Anastasia actually had a suite set aside for him here. The hotel was originally built as apartments for guests of William Randolf Hearst. He knew some mobsters, too.

Headquarters

Overall, social clubs were the choice for headquarters. For instance, the Bergin Hunt and Fish Club at 98-04 101st Avenue in Queens was a mob junction. A certified meeting ground for mobsters. Right out front is where John Gotti held his famous Independence Day celebrations mentioned in chapter 7.

Headquarters could also be in restaurants. Ponte Vecchio (8810 Fourth Avenue, 718-238-6449) had the who's who of the who's dangerous and powerful dining there. Still, headquarters came in all shapes and sizes. They were usually centrally located to the businesses or rackets the particular crew was running. They were found near the main drags: 86th Street in Brooklyn, Tenth Avenue in Manhattan, Mulberry Street in Little Italy. Capos often ran the quarters, and depending on the situation, they were fronted by a working business, whether it was a club, deli, or dart store.

The Bamboo Lounge
Was at Rockaway and Avenue N
Brooklyn

We used to spend a lot of time here. It was a launching pad for burglaries and murders. This is where I first met many of the mob's players. This is also the joint we torched. With all the damn bamboo and straw, it went up in a flash. I was good at torching. You just find the electrical box and use newspaper. Make sure there's a good route for the flames to be the most destructive and bam, insurance.

Fulton Fish Market

Fulton Street and the East River waterfront
* close to the Brooklyn Bridge*
Manhattan

The Genovese family infiltrated the Fulton Fish Market and its seafood. All the families had their fingers in it. I mean, come on, anything with lobster, and we all needed a piece. There were guys here 24/7. Vinny Romano and his brother ran it since the 1970s. Now Vinny and his brother ain't allowed within a mile of the smell. Believe me, it smells down there. If you catch it around 9 or 10 A.M., you can witness sweeping and mopping of fish slime, slicks of it on the pavement. The Fulton Fish Market was 100 percent mob turf. Nothing went down on these docks unless they okayed it. The waterfront and the Gambinos hit the media in late spring of 2002. Peter Gotti was one of over a dozen accused of muscling unions and businesses on the Brooklyn and Staten Island waterfronts. The Genovese family has Manhattan.

Sammy the Bull's Offices

2937 86th Street
Manhattan

The Bull's office occupied a good chunk of the first floor of this building on the side closest to the main corner entrance (now with a red awning). The disco was upstairs. He ran a number of operations out of here on a daily basis. There was fresh coffee and muffins every morning. I'm kidding. The whole Franky Fiale murder took place because of the office. Franky had started moving Sammy's shit out. Note, Franky had not yet even fully purchased the joint or have the okay to move in. Here he was moving Sammy the Bull's personal shit out into the hallway. Plus, he had already put a huge hole in one of the walls for expansion. One night when Sammy confronted him about it, the crazy fuck pulled an automatic weapon on Sammy. That was that.

Lanza Restaurant

168 First Avenue
Manhattan
(212) 674-7014

There were just as many surveillance vehicles as patrons' cars
parked outside. It was a notorious
joint for all the New York families
to meet. The food is still good
here, and so are the "views."

Lindy's Restaurant

825 Seventh Avenue
Manhattan
(212) 767-8343

East New York before paving. 1946 Brooklyn, Pine Street.

Back in the 1920s and '30s, Arthur Rothstein held court here daily.
Have to settle up a debt? See him at Lindy's. Need some advice?
Catch him at Lindy's. You tried to go around him on a score, and
A.R. found out? Don't come within ten square miles of Lindy's.

Mob Classroom

Located in the school across from Rao's
East Harlem

There was always heavy surveillance. We knew it. We fucked with
the cops. One of my favorites was in East Harlem, across from
Rao's. There's an old school that backs up against the FDR. The
cops and feds used a second floor classroom to keep an eye on
the shit going down at the restaurant. These guys would even
dress up like teachers. A bunch of us would yell, "Where's your
paddle, principal prick?" when the fucks were trying to sneak in.
It was fun. Back then, the surveillance equipment was not as ad-
vanced, and it was difficult to get us. They had to work for it. It
was like cowboys and Indians. There was a small mutual respect
that kept the game fun.

Pleasant Avenue

502 East 118th Street at Pleasant Avenue
Spanish Harlem, Manhattan

This avenue is not so pleasant if the Genovese family has a beef with you. Nowadays it's more Puerto Rican than Italian but don't be fooled by the flags hanging from porches. The Italians still pull some weight around here. So much weight it brought Coppola here to shoot the famous scene in *The Godfather* where Sonny (played wonderfully by James Caan) kicks the shit out of his sister's husband with a trashcan for hitting her.

T-Top Triangle

Bordering Shea Stadium
Flushing Meadows, Queens

In a greasy triangular trench in Queens, a long homer from where the Mets play at Shea Stadium (123-01 Roosevelt Avenue), is a tin village, an auto parts hell, a Tijuana Pep Boys. You can spot it from the air when you land at La Guardia. Just look for the scrap piles bordered by Willets Point Boulevard. Drive in here any time of day except Sunday and conveniently unload a stolen car, buy hot parts for cheap, and risk your face getting bashed in with a wrench. This place is sketchy.

Summer Places and Retreats

We needed our little getaways. We led stressful lives. There wasn't a day in my life I didn't live in fear. If that doesn't deserve a little fun, what does?

Massapequa Park

Long Island, New York

If there was part of Long Island that wiseguys favored, it was "The Park." My pal Petey "Sweatband" Scabelli had his spread out here. Pete wore sweatbands for more than just soaking sweat. He was famous for writing cheesy love songs and could never land any girls. Some of the guys feared he'd trick their wives. Carlo Gambino owned an estate here, as well as Gambino capo Roy DeMeo.

Lido Beach
Long Island, New York

You have the Five Towns. Lido was the farthest until you hit Jones Beach. The guys that didn't have year-round homes out here all had summer homes. All the families came out here, but I'd say the Luccheses had the biggest stake. The place was deserted in the winter. You had fucking airline pilots and stewardesses. In the summertime it was insanity. There were beach clubs. If you remember the scene from the film, with Karen and the prick I eventually pistol-whipped, that was out here. Expensive Jewish. It was fucking insane. We owned a joint, the Golden Dome, right over the Atlantic Beach bridge. Paulie and this Jewish guy owned it. The broads, it was unbelievable, everybody snorting coke. The headquarters for all the numbers was on the other side of the club.

"He went upstate" meant the guy got whacked, and don't ask again.

Tommy Lucchese, the old man, lived out here. Johnny Dio had a place out here. Steven Auto, Paulie's cousin, had a house with an elevator in it. The land was so narrow, you were almost either on the bay or on the ocean. From here you could get right into Brooklyn and around on the Belt Parkway straight to Manhattan. It took twenty minutes.

The Azores was Tommy Lucchese's beachfront joint. Paulie's kid, Lenny, was given a job there as a bartender for the summer. Lenny said, "I ain't going to work there unless Henry goes to work there." So they made me maitre d'. Maitre d'! I was twenty-four. Just out of the Army. I had a brand new '64 convertible Bonneville.

Upstate trouble.

Fuck, balls of cash in our pockets. We'd sleep at Paulie's big house on the water almost every night. He had a 45-foot Chris-Craft in the back. The Azores' outside patio went out to the beach. There was dancing and shit, the big bands. Those mornings Lenny and I would wake up on the beach, woo, what I wouldn't do to go back to those nights.

Next was the Lido Beach Hotel. It was the top place to get married, a real nice place. Nowadays for a wedding, hit up the Lido Golf Club (516-889-8181) on the other side, right off Reynolds Channel. The south side is real old Jewish money. The WASP money lived in real palaces on the Gold Coast north, huge spreads with multiple polo fields. Who needs one polo field, let alone two? Me.

The Hamptons
South shore of eastern Long Island

This wasn't as much our spot in my day, but I hear a bunch of the new guys are hitting it now. It's a huge summer weekend party spot. The rich come to rock, and gold-digging city girls come looking to strike it rich. Traffic is bumper to bumper from the city on summer Fridays, so check out the "Cannonball Run," a Hamptons-bound train that leaves Grand Central Friday afternoons. You can even buy booze in the station for the trip and meet people on the ride out. Dune Road is where all the really good shit goes down, those parties you hear rumors about. There's a particular pad named the "castle" at the end of Dune Road where the parties are legendary. Unless you are connected, you'll likely have to stay in the town of Hampton Bays. Try the Budget Inn of the Hamptons' towns, not that it's a slum by any means.

Florida

The east coast of Florida, from West Palm down to the Keys

Trips down here were for business and pleasure. Lots of sunshine, good weather, and loads of drugs and hot goods entering the country. This is where a good chunk of wiseguys vacation and/or have winter homes. I hate the west coast of Florida. We got snagged and arrested in Tampa for beating that prick in the 1970s. Better yet, I was on the agenda to get whacked at the Mohawk Lounge in Tampa in 1980. Guess what? I didn't go.

Hunting Camps

Hunting camps, yeah, I know. Paulie's kid had a place outside of Split Rock, Pennsylvania, one of many mobster hunting camps in the Poconos. There were also hunting (or hunted) camps in the Catskills. We'd head up for doe season, small game season, turkey season, and of course it was always human season. There are a lot of stories of two guys going out, and they'd get a deer, but only one guy came back with the carcass.

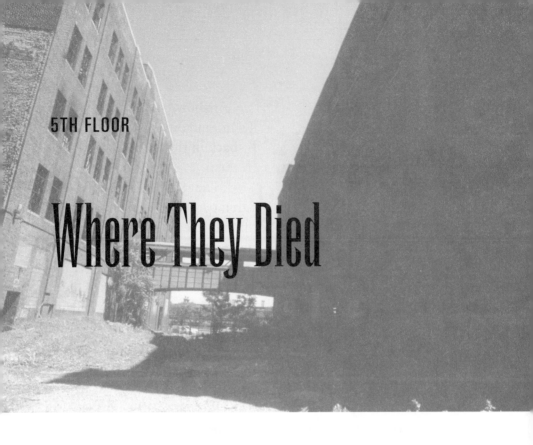

Where They Died

There's no set formula for when and where someone is gonna get it. That's the point: You never know. There are general rules, but even those are broken if you got it coming. To top it off, it's *always* your friends that kill you or set you up to get clipped. In mob life, even a simple insult in a fucking nightclub to a made guy's girlfriend can cost you your life. They'll kill you if you're a rat. Hell, they'll kill you if they got a delusion on you. How can you help that? You can't. To be safe, they'll kill you if you have information to rat, even though they know you likely won't. Basically, you're fucked.

Killings were supposed to be "internal," between ourselves. That was basically bullshit. We tried to follow the skeleton, but all kinds of people got hit. If anyone, cops rarely were killed by us. For one, it brought too much heat. Unlike other cop-hating "gangs," mobsters actually worked together with cops. What good did it do to kill one? There are ten others ready to fill in, like cockroaches. Killing one isn't closing any precincts. It doesn't matter.

A victim of a broken oath.

Anyhow, most cops were moonlighting for the mob back in those days. We needed them.

The Sicilian Oath is, you don't murder in front of one's family members and more important, you don't kill family members. This is bullshit, a fallacy. The mob had a million-dollar hit on my kids and my wife. Some of these fucking rules are really traps for dummies. You buy into this shit, you'll get caught with your pants down.

The first murder I witnessed was Leo the Bookmaker. Bookmaking can be as dangerous as it is lucrative, which I learned at age twelve. Who knows what this guy was up to? Some said he was running junk, as well. He kept saying he needed to get "fixed." At that age, I didn't know the difference between fixing his hair and filling him with junk. He lived on Glenmore Avenue by the train, one block from the pizza joint where I worked. He went to straighten out with somebody, and the guy had this sawed-off shotgun. Leo saw the shotgun coming; I mean he put his hand up. All that did was blow his hand all over his face. Then the shooter pulled out a .32 and shot him in the head but just grazed him. So now you got this bookmaker running around without a hand and a bullet through his head. We heard the shots from the pizza joint, and he comes running up the block. This is the scene in the movie where I get yelled at for wasting aprons. It happened almost exactly like that. The guy lived a few months and died from the poison infection from the shotgun blast.

Here are some of the people who died and the places where the shit went down.

Joe Budha and Frenchy

Corner of Schenectady and Avenue M
Brooklyn
1979

During the murder spree that followed the Lufthansa heist on April 13th, someone looked into a Buick parked at the corner of Schenectady and Avenue M in Brooklyn. Joseph "Joe Budha" Manri and Robert "Frenchy" McMahon were slumped over in the front seat, each shot once in the head with a .44 caliber. This is in the montage footage in *Goodfellas,* although the two bodies fall out of a garbage truck. Either way, they're dead because they knew too much and were promised money from the heist.

Salvatore Maranzano's Office

230 Park Avenue
Manhattan
September 10, 1931

Salvatore Maranzano was the last of the "Mustache Petes," the remaining Old World boss. Not for long. He was the one who devised the five families and then assigned the new kids on the block, the "young turks," to be the rulers. Dumb move. They were about to take him out and take over themselves. You remember how Joe the Boss had his last meal in Coney Island? Maranzano didn't. Hell, it had been six months since that happened. Luciano, one of the "young turks," learned that Maranzano was going to whack him. He knew what he had to do. After learning that the IRS was auditing Salvatore that morning at his 230 Park Avenue office, Luciano had four trusted assassins go perform an audit of their own. Lucky was a sneaky motherfucker. His four hit men disguised themselves as cops there for the audit, rushed the building, and took out the Old Boss' front security. Two "cops" held them while two others stormed the office and shot the Old Boss in a hail of gunfire. They carried the dead weight out and dumped him in

The wire factory a head's roll from the East River.
Stay away from here.

Newark Bay. No body, no crime. That same day, allies of the recently deceased boss went down all over the country. The "young turks" cleaned the slate. The "Mustache Petes" were gone. The new regime was in. Look out.

Kennedy Airport

Annex

1940–present

When those huge jets take off, they make great mufflers for gunshots. Plus, the flashing aviation lights blend with the gunpowder flashes. We would send sorry pricks to their final destination right there on the airstrip. There is still a little maze with scraggly trees and brush back there, straight off Lefferts Boulevard. You could probably go out today and find signs of our rush-job burials. Indentations in the ground, small lopsided mounds of earth, and probably some rusty picks and broken shovels. I haven't been there in over a decade. If that's booked, there's another field south of the airport. Head straight out from Lefferts Boulevard and across the inlet (plan on getting wet) to the far southwestern reaches of the marshy airport property, perpendicular to the JFK Expressway. We weren't the only ones. For years, Murder Incorporated used this area for dumping and disposal.

Market Diner

572 Eleventh Avenue
Manhattan
(212) 695-0415

Still here, the late 1960s' venue of a famous deadly showdown in the parking lot between Jersey and Hell's Kitchen tough guys. Go there today and have a great milk shake or their eggs with Canadian bacon. The fight started in the bar area when one of the bullying Irish Jersey guys asked a Westie for a smoke. Those guys should have stayed in Jersey. One scary tidbit on the Westies: They never, never backed down in their own backyard, no matter what. To keep a fierce and powerful reputation in the neighborhood was more important than the daily scores or nightly whores. The fear and respect Manhattan's West Side paid them was their greatest strength; they made a world with their own rules. Nobody, especially loud, cocky Jersey guys were going to question that authority. After some verbal exchanges, the argument moved outside by the parking lot and turned into a bloodbath. It ended when the cops arrived for the third time, after already escorting the Jersey plates to the Lincoln Tunnel. The entire ordeal included crowbars, tire irons, and a shotgun. Both crews were worked, but the only casualty was a jerk from Jersey who died from a head injury weeks later.

50th Street Underpass

Between Eleventh and Twelfth Avenues
Manhattan

The old New York Railroad tracks still run under 50th Street. You'll notice the heavy fencing and rat poison warnings. Heed these warnings. Stay away from these tracks, especially the under-passes, night and day. They cut down the West Side like a hidden ditch of danger. It's easy to slip in and almost impossible to climb out of. The walls are overgrown with weeds and are ten to twenty feet high. There's a lot of trash and glass and, from what I've heard, a lot of bones. If you went to meet anyone under here, it was probably your last meeting, and you're not reading this. Who can hear you when that damn train goes screaming by? The fucker killing you, that's who. In the 1970s the cops dug it up, a huge media blitz, only to find dog bones.

Robert's Lounge
Lefferts and Rockaway Boulevards
1962–1980

The infamous Robert's Lounge. When you faced the building, the entrance was the door in the middle. The door on the left went up to an apartment we used to play cards and get cocked in. We all had keys and for about ten years were there most days. Jimmy buried over a dozen bodies, including Reno and Spider, under the bocce courts. If you go there today and look down the left side of the building, you'll see the piles of dirt. After I went into the pro-gram, Jimmy had the feds and media over to witness the courts being dug up. There was a single-story dress factory (now a vacant yellow building) next door (to the left facing Robert's), and the bocce courts were behind it. Check it out. Under the club, in the basement, was another graveyard for wiseguys.

The Gemini Lounge
Corner of Troy
Canarsie section of Brooklyn

When Jimmy first introduced me to a couple of the guys from the crew, known as the Gemini Twins, he joked, "When you get hit, these are the guys that are gonna do it." He wasn't really joking. If you haven't read Mustain and Capeci's *Murder Machine,* you need to. It's scary as hell and "executed" extremely well. The Gemini

Nice to see the pigs under the Brooklyn Bridge.
They used to always follow me over it.

Lounge was the kind of neighborhood joint you just might wander into to watch the Jets game with a pal, or grab a frosty mug on a summer evening with the guys. In truth, it was headquarters, especially the apartment behind it, for one of the most brutal crews ever assembled. They had a rep on the street as the most efficient killers in the business. They had committed and disposed of body after body and had it nailed. You cross them you died. You are close to someone that crossed them? You died. Even if you were close to someone that was close to crossing him or her, or better yet, someone they could rip off if he or she suddenly disappeared, goodbye. They used beautiful women to lure their prey. They all had "tool kits" to cut up the bodies. These cowboy fucks got away with it for years.

There's a current Gemini Lounge in Manhattan at 221 Second Avenue (212-254-5260), although very different. It's a good spot for live music, and you'll live to tell about it.

The Cigar Problem

Joe and Mary's Italian American Restaurant
Was at 205 Knickerbocker Street
Brooklyn

Come here today, and you'll see this section of Knickerbocker is a busy street, a business district consisting of several blocks. There are not too many stores open except for fruit markets. The Italian stronghold is long past. Carmine Galante, an ex-Mafia hit man on a quest for absolute power following Gambino's death and Bonanno's retirement, was killing off fellow strong-arms. It was such a bloody quest that the families decided enough was enough. They warned him. He scoffed at their declarations. As you might imagine, his attitude prompted one of the bloodiest assassinations in mob history. Galante was sitting outside, having lunch with a cousin who was leaving town. On the back patio, a hail of bullets from multiple ski-masked men killed everyone out there. "The Cigar" didn't lose his cigar though. Speaking from experience, if they warn you they might kill you, get the fuck out of Dodge or get them first.

The Troutman Shootout

305 block of Troutman between Knickerbocker and Irving
Brooklyn

In 1966, Bill Bonanno was to have a sit-down at the home of Vito Bonventure to discuss Joe. Vito, considered a friend, lived on Troutman, a residential block off a commercial block on Knickerbocker. No meeting took place. Bill Bonanno and his bodyguard were heavily shot at by snipers who were across the street, on top of buildings, and everywhere on Troutman, but they escaped. The only casualties were multiple parked cars and homes. Go there today, and you may be shot at as well. The street looks like a set for a movie about urban warfare. I was there in the daytime in the spring of 2002, and it scared the shit out of me. I didn't get out of the car.

Central Park
Manhattan
Mid-1970s

One of my close associates had met this guy from Atlanta while on vacation in Hawaii. After they got acquainted, this Georgia sucker explained he was looking to score a couple kilos. No problem, says my associate, we can set you up. Set him up they did. They met in Central Park one night in late August. Back in those days, besides a few carriages, the park housed vagrants and evil and was rarely patrolled in the wee hours. In late summer, the leaves ceilinged the park from any moonlight. If you head straight up from Columbus Circle, go up a few hundreds yards or so and take a sharp right, and then go another two hundred yards until it's thick with rocky, hilly terrain. I was there recently, and the whole thing is a fenced-off wildlife refuge. Well, there was no coke, but the Atlanta chap had the money. They buried him right there.

Cypress Garden Restaurant
Was located on Cypress Avenue
Brooklyn

One day when the restaurant was still here, three guys came through the front door and sat down at the third table on the left. The killer entered through the kitchen and littered the table of three with gunfire. The poor fucks, Thomas "Smitty" D'Angeleo and Frankie "Five Hundred," were two of the three killed.

Cuselli's Luncheonette
Eleventh Avenue
Manhattan

On April 19, 1968, Calogero "Charley the Side" LoCicero, a Bonanno member, was enjoying his strawberry malt, enjoying

Typical mob boardroom.

The building on the left was the one from which Irish mobsters
tested human flying with guys that crossed them.

until he was shot repeatedly and died. They say the melting pink
cream and the fresh blood made for an unsettling sight.

Foxy's Last Stand

*Corner of Crossbay Boulevard and Sunrise Highway near
   North Conduit*
Howard Beach, Queens

Foxy was to John Gotti what Tommy was to Jimmy Burke: the
protégé. They called him Foxy because he was the sharpest of
dressers, a couple hundred suits, along with a few hundred pairs of
shoes. Tommy and Foxy had done a lot of scores together. One
score in particular Tommy did alone, though, was start dating
Foxy's sister. She was a looker herself. Her brother did not approve
and let Tommy know. Of course Tommy, the crazy fuck, ignored
him. Then the rumor spread that Tommy had smacked her. Not
good. Foxy cruised by Robert's Lounge all night looking for our

associate. We couldn't do much about it. We were all slaving away with lobster dinners at Lewisburg Federal Penitentiary. Anyway, this was Tommy's personal deal, not our problem. When Tommy heard Foxy was looking for him, he went right to Foxy's apartment. Tommy was not one to back down. This was one of those gated pads, real nice. Foxy comes right up to the gate, opens it, and lands a right fist into Tommy's smug face. Now flat on his back, Tommy pulls out a pistol and gives Foxy two in the forehead and bolts. As the days passed, knowing he was a dead man, Tommy figures he'll turn himself into the cops and try to smooth it out from inside. We had connections and knew we could get him down to Lewisburg with us. Well, he thought everything was cool, but after he got out and they decided to "give the kid a badge," Gotti gave him something different. This all went down while Jimmy and I were in Florida, because they all knew Jimmy would start an all-out war if he were in town. Jimmy would have gotten a machine gun and taken out every Gambino he could find. As they planned, by the time we got back, things had cooled down, and Jimmy had, too.

Gangster Trivia

"Shares grass with the shamrocks" meant the Irish mob was an ally.

Park Central Hotel

870 Seventh Avenue
Manhattan

In the fall of 1928, Arnold Rothstein, the underworld forefather of gambling and loans, found himself dying outside the Park Central Hotel, on the side where the service entrance is. A.R. had gone to meet a friend (supposedly on the third floor) hours earlier. This was another unsolved killing, but there were plenty of rumors why and who did it. Whenever there is gambling, there are debts. You can be killed for owing and being owed. Arnold Rothstein did a lot of both. He was known as a man to pay his debts and collect them. You figure out the rest. He wasn't the last famous mobster to die here. . . .

The Park Sheraton (now the Park Central Hotel)
Was at 55th Street and Seventh Avenue
Manhattan

The barber shop is through the set of double doors forty feet to the left of the main entrance on Seventh.

Just like kids have campfire stories, us gangsters have card-game stories. This is one of them. It was a gloomy October day in 1957, a week before Halloween. The Mad Hatter, Albert Anastasia, was getting one of his frequent trims at his regular spot, the barber shop at the Park Sheraton. As he dozed off during the ritual, two gunmen dressed in all black rushed in and signaled the help away from the chair. Anastasia awoke to look up a barrel. His hand came up but didn't slow down the first bullet. A few more bullets ripped through the boss and through the chair. Glass exploded everywhere; there was blue and red shit spilling all over. He rose, only to drop to the floor from another shot. One of the gunmen finished him off with a bullet into the back of his head, identical to Anastasia's famous 1931 Joe "The Boss" Masseria finale.

There are plenty of theories about why and who killed him. There are those who believe this was simple revenge for the hit on Frank Costello a year earlier. Some say Gambino, knowing as long as Anastasia was alive he would be below him, knew only one way to solve that problem. Others claim Anastasia was bullying into Meyer Lansky's Cuban gambling world. The Mad Hatter's own ego trip ultimately killed him. To remove him from his gambling involvement, Lansky allowed him to be removed altogether. Hey, it may have been all these reasons and more. The gunmen, never caught, are thought to be Joe Gallo and Larry Gallo, although like most good hits, there's no proof.

Lots of blood spilled on these sidewalks, site of Westie mayhem.

Rossini Democratic Club

Irving Avenue
Brooklyn

On April 16, 1968, Francisco Crociata's espresso was interrupted by gunfire. He never finished the espresso, but the gunfire finished him. We used to call a decaf espresso a "Francisco special," because it would knock you on your ass or at least send you to the boys' room.

Sheepshead Bay

Brooklyn

We called it "Creep's-dead Bay." Among many others, Joseph "Joe Jelly" Giorelli took a fishing trip and ended up swimming with the denizens of the deep, because he was a link, a backup shooter in Anastasia's hit. We would go fishing on Paulie's boat out here, and whenever someone snagged a jellyfish, the joke was, it was really the spirit of Joe Jelly. There wasn't a day Paulie invited me fishing I didn't think I was going to join Joe. I hate this bay.

Snoope's Restaurant/Bar
No longer there as Snoope's

The site of Gotti's first hit. The hit was prompted by the Hell's Kitchen Westie James McBratney attempting to make some ransom money by kidnapping Manny Gambino, Carlo's nephew, outta my joint. Not getting the cash, they killed poor Manny. Gotti and a couple other Gambino thugs wrestled him down and then shot him smack-dab during happy hour. It was a messy hit but won a lot of points.

Sparks Flew
Sparks Steak House
210 East 46th Street
Manhattan

In 1985, fierce Gambino capo John Gotti was out of control. He and his crew were breaking a lot of rules, especially in the lucrative smack business. Let me tell you, it's a real cash cow. There was a rumor family boss Paul Castellano was considering "breaking up" the crew. Plus, Paul Castellano had just been indicted on a number of racketeering charges. Some say the family feared he would rat to save his own ass. Sound like anyone I know? Once they have these fears, you're as good as dead. To cure this for his own benefit, Gotti hired a handful of outsiders, dressed them identically, and along with Sammy the Bull, watched "Big Paul" get ambushed outside of Spark's Steak House. The mob boss and his bodyguard Tommy Bilotti were killed. Getaway cars waiting on 47th Street (you can see the carport they drove through, cutting blocks)

Columbus Circle—site of the Colombo slaying.

headed for the tunnels. Why couldn't they let him enjoy one of those juicy steaks before they shot him?

Look Both Ways Before Crossing

Warehouse section of Leonard Street
Brooklyn

On March 11, 1968, Samuel "Hank" Perrone was blown away while crossing the street for smokes from Bingo Warehouse and Trucking Company. He was said to be close to Bill Bonanno.

Manhattan Plaza

43rd Street and Tenth Avenue
Manhattan

In 1981, Henry Diaz, a gambler, was thrown from a window of this apartment complex. Did he die atop a Tenth Avenue parked

We liked classy joints. The Park Central Hotel, 2002.

car? No. He had been dead for a while from knife wounds. Don't fuck with the Westies over gambling—they love bathtubs.

Mazzaro's
2380 Arthur Avenue
Bronx

Summer of 1957, Francesco "Don Ciccio" Scalise, Anastasia's underboss (at the time), was shot repeatedly in this small Bronx market. I have read that the scene in *The Godfather* where Brando gets shot by the fruit market was inspired by this very hit.

No Witnesses on 76th Street
61-05 76th Street
Brooklyn

Michael Consolo, a Bonanno member, was found dead, shot half a dozen times outside his own home. One of the rules is never to kill a guy in front of his family. I guess the loophole is it never said "in front of home." It's all a fucking fallacy—they'd kill your kids if they had to.

"Gone" Zalez
3929 Carpenter Avenue
Bronx
1968

William Gonzalez lived at 3929 Carpenter Avenue in the Bronx. He was shot on his way home. William was an associate of Hank Perrone who had a price on his head, and sometimes just being associated, you find yourself in the same boat.

The Phantom Assassination
15th Street and Fifth Avenue
Manhattan

This is where Carlo Tresca, the famous Italian political refugee who organized the labor strikes of 1912, was taken out. One dark night in January 1943, he was crossing Fifth Avenue to go to a bar from his office with his lawyer/friend Guiseppe Calabi. Out of the night, a quick, almost invisible small figure shot three bullets into Tresca, and I mean right into. The killer was right next to him. A getaway car was on 15th Street facing west, and it sped off into the night. The politician's rumored, but never prosecuted, killer was Carmine Galante. Galante soon became one of the Bonanno Family's most important members. Hey, Guiseppe, so much for defending your client.

Columbo (us) Circle
Columbus Circle
Manhattan
June 28, 1971

Columbus Circle indents the southwest corner of Central Park. Notice the sculpture of the Italian with the world in the palm of

Park Central, formerly The Omni.
Many mobsters have strolled this corridor.

his hands. The Italian flag is painted on the wood at the foot of the central tower. Italians are not shy. Whenever you're lost in New York, you somehow find yourself here at Columbus Circle. There is plenty of traffic, foot and car: a perfect spot for murder.

In the early 1970s, Joe Colombo was bringing a lot of attention to the mob through his Italian Defamation League rallies. Gambino warned him to stop: It brought too much heat. Colombo ignored the warning. Mistake. He was shot three times in the midst of one of his rallies. Cameraman-turned-hired-gunman Jerome Johnson carried out the hit. Colombo's bodyguards then shot Johnson. Too much attention? The murder trial of the Colombo bodyguards was one of the biggest mob trials in history.

Umberto's Clam House
Was originally at the corner of Mulberry and Hester
Manhattan
April 1972

"Crazy Joe" Gallo was turning forty-three. He didn't know this would be his last birthday. He decided to grab a bite and got more than a mouthful. The rule is to never kill a man in front of his family. It was a bad time for the Colombo family. Turmoil actually. Lots of guys were blaming Gallo for the boss's assassination. As far as the family was concerned, Gallo was a dead man. In my opinion, this is where the good days ended. Late on the evening of his birthday, Joey Gallo, with his wife, sister, and others grabbed some late-night grub in Little Italy. As he was eating, three Colombo gunmen barged into the joint and shot him while seated. So much for the Sicilian Oath. Three gunmen rushed in, supposedly tipped by the owner, gangster Matty "The Horse" Ianello. Joe managed to get up from the table after being shot but collapsed outside, dead. No family members died in the shooting.

Neapolitan Noodle House
East 79th Street
Manhattan

Innocent tourists were sometimes mistaken for Colombos by mob rivals and were killed. During the Gallo war, a couple associates spotted some Colombo guys at this crowded Manhattan restaurant. They called the troops in, but by the time they arrived, the Colombo guys had moved on, and some poor suckers got what wasn't meant for them.

Broadway Pub
45th Street
Manhattan

On March 11, the Broadway Pub's manager, Sam Wuack, was murdered by hit men allegedly searching for Genevose capo and bar owner Matty "The Horse" Ianello. Matty the Horse was involved with almost every club and bar worth a shit in the city. He wasn't the easiest guy to track down. So these assassins waltzed right into the joint. "We're coming for The Horse." Most hit men don't wait around a couple hours until the perfect chance. They are in and out. They have their objective and strategy. By the time you see these guys coming, it's too fucking late.

Half Moon Hotel in Coney Island
28th and Boardwalk
Coney Island, Brooklyn

Murder Inc. defector Reles, known as "Kid Twist," got this silly name from his talent of twisting a cord around your neck and killing you immediately. Not so silly anymore. He was a "protected" witness. Despite tight protection, the new witness mysteriously "fell" out the window. They say it was suicide, or because of the Murder Inc. connection, "Jew-icide." Go down to Coney Island in the winter; it's creepy as hell. Make sure not to look under the boardwalk (you'll see the bent fence openings right there as you come up the ramp onto the boardwalk), you won't like what you see. So Reles took the fall and didn't live to tell about it or anything else, which was the point. This is where the saying, "The canary that could sing but couldn't fly" comes from. This hotel is now an old persons' home. (I'll be joining them soon.)

Nuova Villa Tammaro Restaurant
West 15th Street and Boardwalk
Coney Island, Brooklyn
1931

Joseph "Joe The Boss" Masseria and his friend, Charles "Lucky" Luciano, decided to have lunch at one of the day's finest eateries in Coney Island. Well, you have no friends when you are in the higher echelons of the mob. Luciano went for a piss and suddenly four thugs filled Joe the Boss full of holes. Lucky Lucky was taking a leaky. What a coincidence. Yeah right. The gunmen are thought to have been Albert Anastasia, Vito Genovese, and Benjamin Siegel. At the time, household names only in the homes of New York's crime fighters.

Palace Chop and Tavern
(Address? I don't go to Jersey)
Newark, New Jersey

In October of 1935, Dutch Stultz got shot in the stomach in the boys' room by his fellow Murder Inc. murderers. Why? They dis-

The Park Central service door.
Arthur Rothstein's last stand.

agreed with his conviction to bring down Thomas E. Dewey, who at the time was attempting to bring him, and all of organized crime, down. Murder Inc. thought Dewey's assassination would have a negative effect on the whole situation. Dutch's own view definitely had a negative effect on his day. Rumored other reasons Dutch was taken out: He'd become a loose cannon, and he was getting too greedy and being a real prick muscling people around.

Warehouse Blues
Murray Street
Downtown Manhattan

We had this warehouse we used for all our hijacking scores. We pulled right up and unloaded the stuff. One day we pulled up as

Before Joe Valachi wore a wire, others got wired.

usual with a load of televisions and stereos. The foreman, for whatever reason, suddenly started busting our balls. I mean we did this a few times a week without a hassle for years. He asked for our union cards. Jimmy was like, "I'll give you a fucking union card, you prick." Not only did we have a hot load of televisions but also hundreds of tons of cigarettes, razor blades, and vacuum cleaners already stored in the joint. We finally bull-shitted and said we'd bring our cards tomorrow. Yeah right. Next day, Tommy shows up with instructions to shoot him in both kneecaps. Well, he somehow missed the kneecaps and killed the fuck.

The Wire Factory
Deadends 118th Street against the FDR
East Harlem

This now-abandoned wire factory looks scary. Well, it is. The FDR is right there, and the traffic muffles screams and gunshots.

There's wire all over the place, so you didn't need to bring any to slice necks. The grounds surround a deadend in mob central. At least it used to be. Huge rusty fences lined with tarps now imprison the dark deathtrap. I'm sure it's still in use today (not for producing wire).

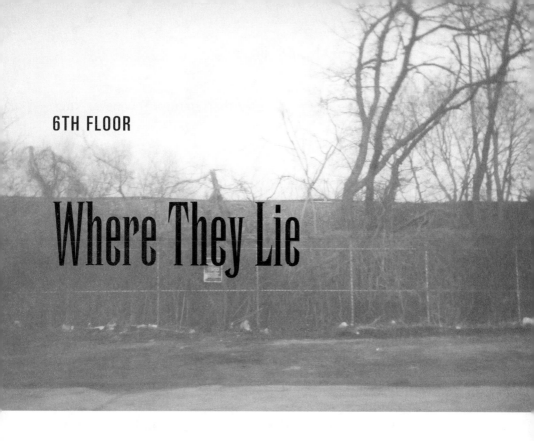

Where They Lie

K nowing where a body lies is as important as knowing who put
it there. Location of the dead could reopen cases, so it was
taken very seriously. If you show any weakness or emotion digging a hole, you might end up in it, too.

Unmarked Graves

For a mobster, the best grave is the one only you and the guy in it
know about. We used rivers, dumps, ditches, dumpsters, freezers,
and straight-up holes. Most of the time, if the hit was planned, the
body was cut or chopped up, which made disposal much easier
and investigating much harder. Hands are cut off. Mouths are
smashed in. Most seasoned guys had the tools of the trade on
them or in their homes at all times. Things like saws, hatchets,
fishing knives, and thick plastic bags were always in reach. There
wasn't a basement in Brooklyn that didn't have quicklime. It

dissolved the corpses much faster than nature. You never knew when you might need it.

50th Street Overpass
Between Tenth and Eleventh Avenues
Manhattan

Under the overpass is the resting grounds for numbers of poor saps on the wrong side of the Westies. There are so many real rats down here, the holes had to be deep. If not, the dog-sized rats would catch the scent and dig the corpse up for breakfast.

Paulie's Scrap Yard
Canarsie, Brooklyn

Paulie's scrap yard had a lot of scraps of flesh. The shit would all get crushed with the cars and sent off to be made into ashtrays. Ashes to ashes, dust to dust . . . there were at least three dozen people who were murdered, tossed into a car trunk, and crushed in the masher at Paul Vario's junkyard in Canarsie. You couldn't tell if stuff was blood, grease, slime, or body parts.

East River (Bottom)
Manhattan

This is where the rumor of "cement boots" began, except it's not rumor. I don't want to know how many five-gallon buckets, in pairs, about shoulder-width apart, are at the bottom of the East River. Believe me, there are plenty. A lot of guys kept boats, and they weren't only for fishing. A lot of guys had buckets, and they weren't for the sandbox.

Fountain Avenue Dump
Canarsie, Brooklyn

This was one of the most popular dumps in town, for bodies that is. Mixed in with the daily tons of garbage were bags of body parts from various crews. Through the 1970s and 1980s the Fountain Avenue eyesore probably consumed hundreds of whacked guys and gals. The staff of the dump was never in on it, but they never asked questions either. Lots of poor fucks had a very informal funeral attended by truckloads of trash.

John F. Kennedy Airport Annex
Queens

Adjacent to Howard Beach, the fields annexing the airport were literally makeshift graveyards for Murder Inc. and our crew, among others. The ground is kind of marshy, very diggable, so rush jobs were cake. If you go out there

A fearsome foursome.

today, although security is a bit tighter, there still are little mounds and broken rusted shovels. Head down Lefferts Boulevard until it ends, you'll come to a security fence, but it's often open. If you get through that, just go straight for a while until you see a little dirt road and some scraggly trees. Yeah, it's creepy, and you'll feel there's something not right. Now look around; you're there.

Madison Square Graveyard (Or Garden)
Manhattan

The cement used to build Madison Square Garden possibly has more corpses or pieces of corpses than any team has players playing basketball or hockey on any given night here. You see, mobsters control construction, and construction sites can be very constructive sites for body disposal. You have all these machines and cement. You cement shreds of body parts and pieces of bone deep in some structure; even if some day they break it up, you'd be long dead. It's not like some whacko deciding to bury his wife in his own basement; this is a fucking giant structure, and the bodies are always at the base. You ever hear Hoffa is in the Meadowlands complex in Jersey? He is.

Mirra Mirra, in the Car

North Moore and West Streets near Pier 25
Manhattan

In 1982, Tony Mirra, as a result of befriending the FBI's agent Joe Pistone, a.k.a. Donnie Brasco, received four shots in the head. They found him in his car in a vacant lot at North Moore and West Streets. Let's just say the Bonnanos were not happy with him.

Robert's Lounge Bocce Courts

Lefforts

Do you remember when Pesci's character in *Goodfellas* shot the kid Spider (played wonderfully by *The Sopranos'* Michael Imperioli) during a card game? That happened, and under the bocce courts behind Robert's Lounge is where he was buried, among others. Years later, after all the shit went down with me going into the program, Jimmy had the courts dug up for the cops, and no bodies. If you stop by, you can't get in the place, but if you stand facing it, look down the left side, and you can still see the piles of dirt. They're still there, I'm just not sure where the bodies are now.

Gangster Trivia

A tribute is money that you shoot to your superiors, even in other families, to show your respect and loyalty after a score.

Sonny Black's "Toll" Paid

South Avenue
Staten Island

The body of Dominick "Sonny Black" Napolitano was discovered in the creek near the bridge here in 1982.

Following Donnie Brasco's coming-out party, the man who was held responsible for letting him rise so high was found close to the Geothals Toll Bridge on Staten Island. Because of him

bringing a fed into their world, when they found him he was missing his hands. Legend has it he gave his jewelry to his crew before
he had to attend a "meeting."

Tommy Desimmone's Backyard

115th Avenue and Lefferts Boulevard
Brooklyn

True in the film, although the name in the movie was DeVito,
Tommy's mother did live in the area, although he was rarely at
home (he had an apartment above Robert's Lounge and another
place with his wife). Yet he did use the backyard for burying
quite a few whack-jobs that are probably still down there, what's
left of them.

Washington Square Park

Manhattan

I don't go near this place at night. Why? Because it's fucking
haunted. I'm serious. In the old days, guys used to slip a late-night
corpse in here. The scariest part isn't the old mobsters but the fact
they're joining thousands and thousands that were hung from the
very trees there, then buried on the spot. No wonder the grass is so
nice. Stay away at night, unless you're trying to scare a broad back
to your hotel. It's good for that.

Ward's Island

A notorious body dump for the Westies, that ruthless Irish Gang
from Hell's Kitchen. They had a contact at the sewage treatment
plant out there, and he would let them add the already-cut-up
body parts to the sewage. The only thing the contact insisted on
was seeing the face of the victim. I guess he got off on seeing the
expression. Then he'd take it from there, into the plant. A bit of an
Irish stewage. Where did they go? I know for a fact some of them
went into the river, especially the bodies that hadn't been chopped
up. To really sink a full corpse, you need to puncture the lungs and
stomach, open it up. The currents around the island are so strong,

Brooklyn and Queens' funeral homes
make a killing off the mob lifestyle.

some say a body won't surface until it gets to Montauk at the end
of Long Island.

West Side Rail Yard

Low 30s bordering Tenth Avenue near the Chelsea Pier
Manhattan

This massive railyard has more than tracks and rail, it has rolling
heads, arms, legs, and complete battered corpses. Sometimes they
weren't buried. Sometime they weren't dead yet. Oh, but those
were buried. This was the handiwork of the out-of-control wild
fucks, the Irish Westies. These guys were so fucking crazy. They
didn't abide by the rules, because they had none. Plenty of poor
saps were killed for no other reason than that they bumped into a
Westie at a bar.

Marked Graves

New York has more people than any other city in the United States. New York also has more dead people than any other city in the United States. Especially if you fly into La Guardia, all you see are graves. Sprawling headstone skylines dwarfed by the backdrop of the city itself. By American standards it's an old city. The history is rich, almost as rich as some of the deceased, so there is no shortage of impressive family memorials, many of them were Catholic.

Those guys that die of old age, you'll see below, shock the shit out of me. You get into that life, and you will most likely die from it. Membership is for life, or death. I was going to die. There was a hit on me, from one of my best friends. It was going to happen at the Mohawk Restaurant in Tampa. I was supposed to go down there for a "job." The job was *me*. I should be at one of the cemeteries listed here. They are some of the most expensive addresses in the World of the Dead.

It is so appropriate. You can go find the graves of those who put so many others in theirs. New York has absolutely beautiful cemeteries. Most offer tours, and as you'll find, gangsters aren't the only famous corpses in the Big Apple.

MOUNT HEBRON CEMETERY

130-04 Horace Harding Expressway
Queens
(718) 939-9405

Emanuel (Mendy) Weiss
Block 115, Lot 8, Ref. 1, Grave 10

Mendy was one of three Murder Inc. demons to die in the arms of the electric chair at Sing Sing, on the night of March 4, 1944. That chair was as notorious as the gangsters that died in it. You heard all these stories that it used to talk to you before you died. It would whisper in the voices of all the other men who took their last seat and died before you. I guess the toughest, craziest fuckers, guys who had faced death on the street dozens of times, would just start freaking out, like something was biting them inside their ears. I don't know how this shit got started, since no one lived to tell about it, but the story always scared me. Maybe it was a way to sway youngsters from following the path of their neighborhood heroes.

Louis "Lepke" Buchalter

This guy had balls. Lepke was the leading labor racketeer of the 1930s and 1940s. This infamous Jewish mob boss was pals with Lucky Luciano. His turf was the garment district. Lepke's most famous order was the Dutch Shultz contract. Dutch was one of theirs, but he insisted they put a contract on the New York D.A., Thomas Dewey, who was bringing down mobsters all over town, especially targeting Dutch. Lepke refused Dutch's request, which Dutch refused to accept. Buchalter knew the mob would be in trouble from the added heat and lack of sympathy that Dewey's murder would invite, so the only answer was to take out Shultz.

Gangster Trivia

Bugsy Siegel borrowed $5 million in Brooklyn-based Murder Inc. money to build the Flamingo Hotel and Casino, Vegas' first supercasino. He lost the money, then lost his life because of it.

Martin (Buggsy) Goldstein
Block 42, Ref. 3, Sect. D, Grave 26

Goldstein was another victim of the Sing Sing electric chair and a success story for law enforcement. He was part of Murder Inc. running out the back of the Midnight Roses candy store in Brownsville, Brooklyn. His heyday was the 1930s. As far as Jewish mobsters go, he was fairly low in the hierarchy, but I know from experience, you can still have a good time at that level.

SAINT JOHN'S CEMETERY

8001 Metropolitan Avenue
Queens
(718) 894-4888

Frank "The Dasher" Abbundando
Block 115, Lot 8, Ref. 1, Grave 10

One of Murder Inc.'s "kids" died February 19, 1942. He too took his last gasp of air in the grip of the Sing Sing Prison electric chair. They called him the Dasher because he did most of his murders on foot, and he was quick as death himself.

Joe Colombo
Section: 36, Range F, Plot 2, Grave 1

Joe Bonanno, during the so-called Banana Wars, ordered hits on some of the top mob bosses in the business, namely, Lucchese and Gambino. The crazy fuck. It was a good plan until his go-to hit man, Joe Colombo, decided to let the targeted bosses know. This brought Joe Colombo up a few notches, and when the time came to fill Joe Profaci's dead shoes, he was the man. The family was renamed after him, and Joe stayed the boss of it until 1971. This was the famous Columbus Circle hit that they say Carlo Gambino ordered.

Neill Dellacroce

Dellacroce was underboss of the Gambino Crime Family under Carlo Gambino and then under Paul Castellano. He died a natural death, but his death is said to have caused the famous Parks Steak House Ambush, which happened a few months after his demise. Dellacroce was one of the most trusted and effective underbosses of the most successful crime family ever. His death triggered events that got out of hand. After Gotti got his way, his new underboss,

In Howard Beach, just drive to the end of 115th to the tracks. Those trees aren't the only dead things here. We disregarded the NO DUMPING sign.

Frank DeCicco, was blown up by a car bomb (supposedly intended for Gotti himself) a few months after Sparks Steak House.

Carmine Galante

They called him "The Cigar" because he loved them to his death. This fucker was ruthless. I'm telling you the stories on the street about this guy. When he came out of jail, no one wanted anything to do with him. He was a hit man and drove for Bonanno before Bonanno left for Arizona. When he took over the reins, he thought he was gonna run everything, everyone. His famous line was, "Who among you is going to stand up to me?" Next thing you know, he's laying down in a pool of blood at Joe and Mary's restaurant in Brooklyn, cigar in his mouth. He was murdered on July 12, 1979, right before I retired from the mob myself.

Carlo Gambino

One of the most famous mobsters of all time, America's "boss of bosses." His climb to the top began in the early days with two other "young turks," Anastasia and Luciano. Gambino was small and unimposing, which he knew gave him a different hand to play with. The sharp Gambino worked his way to the top, all the while dodging the law and his fellow bosses. He walked among the people daily as a well-liked, often worshipped figure of the Italian community. He died naturally at his home.

Vito Genovese

This famous boss planned more botched hits than any mobster I've heard of. What luck. He hired "The Chin" to kill Frank "King of Slots" Costello. The Chin missed. A pissed, bullet-grazed-headed Costello had a good idea of which greedy underling was responsible. Still Genovese was a respected and feared man. He was rumored to be responsible for keeping the FBI officially out of all of organized crime's affairs for many years, a custom that Costello started. Genovese walked between the raindrops until he died in prison on February 14, 1969. You'll notice there is a drugstore in New York City with the same name. The Genovese family ran a lot of drugs no doubt, but not the kind the Genovese well-stocked pharmacies carry nowadays.

John Gotti

There is a family mausoleum. Gotti died in June of 2002 of natural causes in the prison hospital.

Gotti was known as many things other than a boss, especially to those inside. The public knew him as the "Teflon Don" for all the cases he beat and the "Dapper Don" for his sharp suits. The guys I talked to knew him as a guy that took on too much responsibility and too much spotlight. When I was first introduced to Gotti, he was smacking some guy over the head with a bat. He was sixteen, one of those young punks that backed down to nobody. I mean nobody. He was an enemy you didn't want to cross. He earned his stripes on the street by taking part in the James McBratney hit. After a jail sentence for that, he ran as a capo out of the Bergin Club, then as a boss out of the Ravenite. His impressive burial service may have been the last of the great mob funerals.

Gangster Trivia

In the mob, getting coal in your stocking meant you were disappearing over the holidays, or a warning to lay low. The holidays were a time of celebration … and killing. It was easier since lots of people were out of town and/or drunk. No one knew you were missing until mid-January.

With the environment in mind,
we fertilized the fragile wetlands of JFK Airport with dead bodies.

Wilfred "Wahoo" Johnson

They called him Wahoo for two reasons: one he had Indian blood, two he was crazy as a hoot owl. I knew he was crazy when I heard he ratted on Gotti as one of the government's star witnesses. He refused to enter witness protection. On top of that he stayed in Brooklyn! He was crazy. On August 29, 1988, eighteen bullets met Wahoo in front of his Brooklyn home.

Salvatore "Lucky Luciano" Lucania

They called him "Lucky" because in the 1920s Salvatore Maranzano, one of the two New York "Mustache Pete" bosses, had Luciano supposedly beat to death and thrown in a river out on Staten Island. Luciano wasn't dead, though, hence the nickname. His legend lives on as perhaps the greatest gangster of all time. I couldn't agree more. He was a progressive thinker born out of the Prohibition era and was against the old ways of earning. He was an ambitious criminal businessman and understood what needed to be done. He was so influential, the government had to go to him for help during World War II when they feared a German U-boat invasion of New York. He died January 26, 1962.

Harry "Happy" Maione
Section 37, Range L, Grave 1

Happy was another of the famed Murder Inc. squad. I heard this guy never wiped the smile off his face, and what made him the happiest, well, you don't want to know. He died in 1942.

Salvatore Maranzano
Section 25

What I love about his setup is Maranzano's killers are buried almost next-casket-door to his. The chap that set up the hit was Lucky Luciano. It was 1931, and they found the body in Newark Bay, following that cop-disguised ambush in Maranzano's own Brooklyn office. I heard this guy was a real hard ass in his living years. Not the kind of guy you want to share a beer with.

He was from Castellemmare del Gulfo in Sicily, as were many of the founding American wiseguys. He was part of the struggle for absolute underworld power called the Castellemmare Wars. It's said he was one of the most educated of any mobster, not that that's saying a lot. Most of my associates finished ninth grade if they got that far.

James Napoli
Section 39

One of the sharpest mobsters to ever live. He was a capo for the Genoveses as long as I can remember. This fucker knew how to make money gambling. I met him on a few occasions. Nice guy, but I knew whenever you meet guys like this, you're gambling with your life. He ran a bunch of shit and ran it well. Running a tight ship in the mob means tight lips, a quick trigger, and your guns always have silencers, as in no one hears about it. Napoli lived it out and died peacefully in the 1990s.

Joseph Profaci

He was called the "Olive Oil King" because of all the damn olive oil he brought into the country. He was notoriously greedy, and everyone knew he was a prick. He was the other side of the Gallo war I mention in the movie. Before it was like the golden age of wiseguys, to me at least. I was still pretty young, just getting out of the army and back into things when the Profaci-Gallo War broke out. Profaci was such a prick that a fucking war broke out because he was hoarding the "hard-earned" money of his crew, and the Gallo brothers couldn't take it anymore. They wanted to whack him, but he managed to die himself from health issues on June 6, 1962. Joe Colombo took over from there.

Philip "Rusty" Rastelli
The Cloisters

This guy had a life. He was boss of the Bonanno Family twice and was shot by his wife/crime partner with more than one bullet because he cheated on her. Rusty was one of the few gangsters to successfully run the camp from prison. He died from cancer in a Queens hospital in the early 1990s.

Frank "Funzi" Tieri
The Cloisters (just ask for the Wood Section)

One of those crazy fucks that lived through hell, dying naturally. He was boss of the Genovese family in the 1970s. Anthony "Fat Tony" Salerno was in the batter's box and went to bat in 1981 when Funzi bit it.

ST. MICHAEL'S CEMETERY

72-02 Astoria Boulevard
Astoria, Queens

Frank "King of Slots" Costello

Costello was the "Prime Minister" of the mob. His fingers were in places you didn't even think fingers could get near. The helpful guys were all in his pocket: cops, ministers, mayors, senators, even the FB fucking I. His contacts are why star witness "Kid Twist" Reles took his famous Coney Island flight to the death. Costello was for more head power, less gunpowder. People were always trying to kill him though. "The Chin's" bullet came within inches of early retirement. Rest in peace? Not Frank. Someone later broke into his burial crypt and disturbed the corpse while looking for valuables. Genovese blew the crypt open to signal he was not into the old ways. What a prick. Costello was to the mob what George Washington was to America. All the new wiseguy kids today should have to pass a quiz on the old bosses before getting a button.

GREEN-WOOD CEMETERY

500 25th Street
Brooklyn
(718) 768-7300

Green-Wood is beautiful and peaceful. Unlike its residents, Crazy Joe Gallo and Albert Anastasia.

Albert Anastasia

"The Mad Hatter" because of his unusual head fashions. This guy, one of the "Young Turks," is easily one of the most famous mobsters ever. He was said to be the main executioner in Murder Inc. This guy was a real bad ass.

Gangster Trivia

Candy, markers, ammo, liners, stocking stuffer, sweetener, garnish, and pledges are all terms for cash.

MORAVIAN CEMETERY

2205 Richmond Road
Staten Island
(718) 351-0136

Tommy Bilotti

Plot is to the right of Big Paulie's mausoleum

Tommy was the acting underboss to Castellano when they were shot at Spark's Steak House in Manhattan. Said to be a loyal friend to Castellano. Their murders were ordered by John Gotti and Sammy the Bull Gravano.

Paul Castellano

Lying in an unmarked crypt on the second tier of the main mausoleum here is the body of Paul Castellano, the nephew of Carlo Gambino and one of the few mobsters to gain similar respect. He ran the Gambino family until Gotti's men took him out at Sparks. "Big Paulie" lived up on Todt Hill on Staten Island. This guy knew how to live. They called his house "The White House."

Frank DeCicco

This is the guy that set up big Paulie for the hit at Sparks. He got his a few months later when his car blew up. Franky always seemed like a good guy when I met him on a few occasions. The fact is, once you're a mobster, you're a mobster, and that's it. Big Paulie was supposed to be a "great guy," but business is business.

Clubbing, Without a Bat

There are mobbed-up joints and there are joints that mobsters love. We frequented both. Public establishments don't have the luxury of saying what kind of folks can and, more important, what kind of folks can't enter. So what if some may hold the right to refuse service. The places we're talking about aren't exactly the kind you want to refuse anything. That in mind, the clubs I list aren't mob-affiliated but are rumored to be mob-frequented. These guys aren't gonna fuck with you either. Not to say it never happens, but they don't want to get any added heat because of some chump from out of town. Just mind your business, and you're good. If hot-shot mobsters have a thirst for going somewhere, it probably means the place is off the hook. Remember, wiseguys, like most guys, like swanky spots, hot broads, good times, good service, and opportunities. They also like to mingle with the stars and starlets when possible. So often, the same place you see a ton of super-model figures, you'll find organized crime figures. Not a bad setup. So dive in and enjoy.

We didn't have offices with receptionists. We liked to keep a lot of our real business away from our legit biz. Clubs and lounges were for just that. Oh, and for the booze and broads. Families usually didn't own these places. They just took them over, claimed them. Private clubs, too. Nothing is exempt. Don't care if Donald Trump owns it, they'll cause heart attacks with the unions and bullshit until they get a piece of the joint.

There were even cop clubs where the cops and agents would hang out after surveilling all of us hanging out. Sometimes we'd end up at the same place, competing for the same broads. We always got the broads. Most of the beefs started at the hot swinging joints; there'd be two or three different crews. Someone would insult somebody's broad, all those egos mixed with alcohol. Trouble.

Everyone wants to get lucky during the visit, especially when married. What else are visits for? In the big city, you have to beware. Trust me, I used to set guys up. If there was someone we needed or we wanted to get something from them, we'd just go to Bobby "Murgy the Pimp" Monroy. Murgy wasn't a pimp by trade; he was a bookie full-time and worked at his pop's insurance company, but he knew a ton of heartless hotties that would do anything for the right price. Women just adored and trusted him. I could never figure it out. He was a pale-skinned, dark-haired devil, sporting knickers and a sport coat most days, creepy at best. Murgy spent most of his time shaking people down for bets by the Flatiron Building on Fifth Avenue. He set us up with one of his girls. He never failed. We'd send these girls in anywhere. They could deliver any guy after just an hour or two in the bar with them, right into our ride. Nothing deflates a boner faster than realizing what just happened. Don't sell yourself short, but

Gangster Trivia

Mob girlfriends, I've read, are called "goumadas" and "comares." I didn't hear this much. We referred to them as "girlfriends."

if some 10 is all over you out of the blue, don't leave the bar with her alone if possible. If not, hell, risk it.

Most of the joints we hit are long gone. Nightclubs just don't stand the test of time. There's so much corruption in the business, how could they? The following is a list of some of the newer spots, some of the late spots, and some of them that are still around.

Out of New York, which means eating shittier food.

Café Carlyle
35 East 76th Street
Manhattan
(212) 570-7189

This is my kind of place, old-school class. Chances are, every Monday you'll most likely catch a famous New Yorker and Hollywood director playing sax.

Cecil's Discothèque
54th Street
Manhattan

No longer here, this place went off. Guys from all the families went here, even guys in from Buffalo. Cecil's was a well-known, mob-frequented joint. When Joe Pistone was sliding into his successful role as Donnie Brasco, he hit this spot religiously to get his mug shown around the underworld.

Copa Cabana
617 West 57th Street between Eleventh and Twelfth Avenues
Manhattan
(212) 582-2672

The memories here. It's still a great place if you're into Latin women. This place had the best acts.

Back in the late 1960s, every Friday night was for the girlfriends, and this was not just the Luccheses or our crew. All the families had guys who took part in this. It was a dangerous situation, if you got caught staring at some hothead's broad, everyone in the joint had "pistol-dick." Pistol-dick was how we'd stuff the gun down the front in case there was light frisking.

Cotton Club
656 West 125th Street at Twelfth Avenue
Manhattan
(212) 663-7980

Yes, this is *the* Cotton Club. The legend lives on. We used to hit it up on Saturdays once in a blue moon. This was obviously not the kind of place a guy like me wanted to wander into back then, but Stacks (played by Samuel L. Jackson in *Goodfellas*) dragged me down there, and it was some of the best shit I've ever witnessed.

Culture Club
179 Varick Street
Soho, Manhattan
(212) 243-1999

This popular venue wasn't around in my day, but the music was. Step back to 1980. The only difference is the girl you're dancing next to has better hair.

Post-Air France robbery celebration. I'm first on the right, in my lower 20s.

Eden
28 West 20th Street
Manhattan
(212) 627-7867

This property, like most of the people here, is absolutely beautiful. Flowers, waterfalls, don't forget your Eve, Adam, unless you are a stud.

Float

240 West 52nd Street
Manhattan
(212) 581-0055

Like to dance? This is the place where the dancing goes from the floor, and if you're good enough, back to your hotel room.

Hippopotamus

61st Street and York Avenue
Manhattan

I have never been here. If I stepped in there in its early '80s reign, I would have been killed in ten minutes tops. This was the old dance club known as the dancing mobsters' wet dream. Joe Pistone knew this when he wanted to show his face around the faceless. Everyone knew about this place.

Lansky Lounge & Grill

104 Norfolk between Delancey Street and Rivington
Manhattan
(212) 677-9489

Right out of a gangster flick. This Lower East Side drinks-sometimes-dinner spot is a former speakeasy the "chairman of the board" Meyer Lansky used to frequent. Lansky had the final word in any contract that was in front of Murder Inc. You have to check this place out. You can't miss the sign, but the entrance is hidden in the alley—just like the old speakeasy days. Yes, you can go there today, and it's still a hotspot, even without prohibition.

Limelight

660 Sixth Avenue at 20th Street
Manhattan
(212) 807-7780

If the walls of the Limelight of my day could talk, oh my. It was always on our list, especially if we were short a few dames. I knew a bunch of the bartenders, and they always took care of me. Plus, it's laid out like a maze, so if you play your cards right, you can sneak away with a fox you met on the floor and leave your date in the dark.

Good news, too, the Limelight is back on.

Lot 61
550 West 21st Street
Manhattan
(212) 243-6555

I was here recently, and the girls outnumbered the boys two to one and were ten times as cute. Get here early unless you know someone at the door, or inside the door, because there are long lines (which you may find in the washrooms as well). Hey, it's New York, this shit goes on everywhere. Places can't help the fact patrons have nostrils.

Bar in Morgan's Hotel
237 Madison Avenue
Manhattan
(212) 726-7600

Ian Schrager again attracts hotel guests and locals to his hotel's bar. The decor, staff, and guests are delicious, and the drinks aren't bad either.

One51
151 East 50th Street
Manhattan
(212) 753-1144

One of the places celebs, want-to-be celebs, and want-to-see celebs mingle and turn suddenly single. I fucking love it. Big up-and-comers in the industry come here. To make things even better, it's a classy joint with a good vibe. The music's a little hip for a guy my age, but I'm not the only one my age in there.

Once Sammy the Bull's infamous "Suite" nightclub.

Pen-Top Bar and Terrace
700 Fifth Avenue at 55th Street in the Peninsula Hotel
Manhattan
(212) 956-2888

On the twenty-third floor of the ritziest hotel that's not the Ritz, you'll find some of the highest class "ladies" you've ever laid eyes on. Get over here. Pen-Top is at the top of the drink chain in New York. Grab your credit card and your best digs and dig in.

Rainbow Room
30 Rockefeller Plaza, sixty-fifth floor
Manhattan
(212) 632-5000

If you want to step back into the glory days of my life, the brighter side of the dark side, dress to the nines and head over to this Rockefeller Plaza gem. This joint has always been well-known not for its mob affiliation but for its mobster frequentation, as well as a rotating dance floor. It's a classy spot with beautiful broads, always a welcome change from the musty social clubs of Brooklyn and Queens.

Rise

2 West Avenue in the Ritz-Carlton Hotel
Manhattan
(212) 344-0800

Drink prices are not the only things that rise here. Wait until you see the broads.

Suite 16

127 Eighth Avenue
Manhattan
(212) 627-1680

Actors, actresses, cages to dance in, and the best deejays, all ingredients for a good time. All the while, you have the feeling you are in a plush hotel room. They even have mini-bars. Hey, if nothing else, you can pretend for a moment there are a bunch of hotties in your hotel room.

Gangster Trivia

Steve Kaplan paid off the Gambino crime family, at the time led by the Dapper Don, to protect his Atlanta Gold Club. Rumors still fly about the 1997 hotel sex romp with female employees of the club and the New York Knicks.

Alleged Mafia Social Clubs and Some of Their Alleged Social Events

Social clubs can be very antisocial to outsiders. You just don't waltz into these joints asking guys if they're "made" or how many "hits" they've accumulated. Nonetheless, it's the best way to see the real deal.

Bergin Hunt & Fish Club
98-04 101st Avenue
Queens

I'm sure you've heard all the stories about this place. Last I checked, it's still there. Stay put and stay alive. Gotti ran out of this place as a capo before he knocked off Big Paul. Gotti's funeral came right by here in June 2002, proof this place is still connected.

Friday night at the Copa. Don't ask about the suit.

Tommy Collin's Club
722 Tenth Avenue
Manhattan

Site of the long-gone Hell's Kitchen backroom-gambling spot. You can still see the steps that led to the door.

Diplomat Social Club
Was at Third Avenue and Carrol Street
Brooklyn

You had to be diplomatic in here, or you would die.

The notorious social club was the longtime headquarters for the Colombo crime family. The jukebox was always played loudly: 1) so it could be heard by the feds listening in, 2) so that's all they heard.

The Gemini Lounge
Troy Avenue
Canarsie, Queens

The media knows the Gemini Lounge as well as anyone. Roy Demeo's crew, under the Gambinos, functioned as one of the most murderous crews ever to hold court in New York. Most of the killing happened in the apartment behind. The entrance was on the side of the corner bar, near the air-conditioning vent.

Little Italy.
A lot of mobsters

Motion Lounge
Graham Street
Greenpoint, Brooklyn

Social club run by Bonnano capo, Dominick "Sonny Black" Napolitano. In the film *Donnie Brasco*, he was the character with pigeons. In reality, Sonny Black did in fact have pigeon cages on top of the club. He bred racing pigeons. "Sonny Black" took a one-way trip to Staten Island because of it.

Murder Inc. Headquarters
700 block of Saratoga
Brownsville, Brooklyn

The front was Midnight Rose's Candy Store, in the back was the contractual demise of hundreds of lives. If you go there today, you'll see the yellowish train underpass on Saratoga. The headquarters is very close to the underpass.

Robert's Lounge
114-45 Lefferts Boulevard (Lefferts and Rockaway)
Brooklyn

Last I heard, this place was for sale. You'll see a huge old telephone company building. You can't miss it: There are no windows, and it's uglier than me. This was my hood. Robert's was our place. This is where we came to settle scores and start them. It was a bet's throw from Aqueduct Raceway, and the back had bocce courts. Upstairs was an apartment. Our crew ran the place.

Toyland
94 Hester Street
Manhattan

Nicky Marangello's (ex-Bonanno underboss) social club. It was a hub for all the families, but still the Bonannos' joint. You wanted to get into business with them in the 1980s? You had to come here.

Hawaiian Moonlighters Club
140 Mulberry Street
Little Italy, Manhattan

Don't let the happy sweet name fool you. This place was as scary as places get. Smack-dab in the middle of Little Italy, it was the ultimate mob lair. I have never been to this address and will never go.

596 Club
Was at 43rd Street and Tenth Avenue
Manhattan

This is the infamous bar that Irish mobster poster child Jimmy Coonan owned. It later was called T-Bags. A lot of blood has spilled on these floors. It's a whole book in itself (*The Westies* written by T.J. English—amazing book). In 1982, a bartender, Tommy Hess, happened to hit this Irish guy's ex-girl one night. That Irish guy happened to be a Westie named Richie Ryan. Woops. Richie came in, pistol-whipped, then pulled the bartender's pants down, stuck the revolver up his ass, and did the deed. Holy crow, they were fucked up!

The Ravenite
Was at 247 Mulberry Street
Little Italy, Manhattan

More bugs than a Canarsie marsh in August. Was run by Gambino Neil Dellacroce. Gotti used to spend a lot of time here, almost daily. That was great for the Organized Crime Strike Force. Gotti demanded weekly meetings with every captain. Failure to show up got you killed. Most showed up. This was an unexpected treat for the feds, 'cause there Gotti is, kissing cheeks right there on the sidewalk, to the same unknown cats week in and week out. The guys that had been under the radar for years were now on the feds' list. That was the big difference between Castellano and Gotti: common sense. All of a sudden, the whole Gambino operation, boss on down, is being mapped out because of the predictable showings Gotti set up. I should say he set himself up. When he wasn't greeting his crews on the street, he was talking too much in the apartment above the club (which was also bugged). That's where the court got some of that recorded famous Gotti commentary. All in all, the Ravenite was the site that single-handedly brought down the Gambinos under Gotti.

Triangle
208 Sullivan Street
Manhattan

I've heard people call this spot the "Borough-muda Triangle" because of all the fuckers that just "vanish" when they say they are going here.

Victory Star

311 East 76th Street
Manhattan

There are few victories here unless you're from the neighborhood, or your brother is.

Arlington

391 Manhattan Avenue
Brooklyn

Pittsburgh Paul enjoying New York's nightlife and Pittsburgh's drugs.

I swear this place was named after the Arlington Cemetery. Can you guess why? A lot of crews ran out of this place. I never step foot in here and never will. Too many stories, not happy ones.

Banner

7509 New Utrecht Avenue

The banner reads "Do not enter."

Café Silicia

6415 Bay Parkway
Brooklyn

Guys used to sing a mob version of the S&G New York classic. Instead of "breaking my heart," they used "breaking my balls." This place was a great one to get your balls literally broken in.

Seamens

469 Myrtle Avenue
Brooklyn

There were more gunmen than seamen. Do not go looking for this place.

Veterans and Friends Club
Bay Ridge, Brooklyn

Was a couple doors down from Tomasso's Restaurant. The notorious Gambino haunt where Paul Castellano and Carlo Gambino spent much of their time with their family. I am referring to their criminal families. It's where guys checked in, and sometimes checked out, a couple doors down from the famed restaurant.

Out in front on April 13, 1986, Frank DeCicco's car blew up. So did most of Frank. Word on the street is the bomb was meant for John Gotti, a little plan Vinny "The Chin" Gigante conspired. You see, we never used bombs. It was against the rules. Gigante knew they'd be less likely to suspect an Italian because of the explosives. They ended up tracing the shit to Florida and back up to Gigante, or so they say.

The Suite
111-16 Queens Boulevard
Forest Hill, Queens

This is the joint I owned in the 1970s right off Queens Boulevard. You'll see there's a little business/service road that parallels the main drag. The Suite was on that, next to a stone building that was a health club. A couple blocks away was A Touch of Class, another mob hub. It was a convenient location, right before the 59th Street Bridge in Forest Hills. Also convenient for nearby jockeys from Aqueduct or Belmont to score some coke. The place was hopping for a while, and we were selling a lot more than food and booze.

Now it's a really good sushi restaurant, and it's still there. If you walk into the restaurant, the layout's different, but if you look on the right, the bar is basically in the same place. If you recall the film *Goodfellas*, this is where Joe Pesci's character, Tommy, is getting his balls busted by Billy Batts, the made guy, and they kill him. This is where the real thing went down. Just like that. I locked the door, and it's in the same place it was that night.

My joint was actually really safe. Things got a little rowdy once in a while. Me, Jimmy, and a few other guys had gotten really cocked one night and just turned the place over. Next morning, the old lady comes in and she sees the place is turned over, trashed. Everyone gets hysterical and starts telling me, "The feds were here" or "Someone's crew." Little did they know, it was us dumb drunks that did it. Why? We were crazy assholes.

Café Espresso

2339 Arthur Avenue
Bronx

Do not come looking for this place for your own, and your family's, safety. This isn't some yuppie coffee joint where you sit around and read the *Village Voice*.

Corleone Social Club

3205 Westchester Avenue
Bronx

This a mob spot? No way.

Gangster Trivia

If one mob member is attacked, it is considered an attack on all members. This rule bends all different ways.

Plaza Suite

2937 86th Street
Queens

This was Sammy the Bull's club. Upstairs was a disco, downstairs was Sammy's offices. The building's still there, but go there today and you'll see it's a completely different business (think Disney movie about a deer). Franky Fiale was trying to buy the club. He was crazy. He was some Czech coke dealer. Crazy as rat shit. He was the one who was out of his mind and moved into Sammy's office. Not a good move. On top of that, this crazy coked fuck pulled out an uzi when Sammy confronted him. Same night, Franky got both his eyes shot out in the parking lot on the corner of the Plaza by Sammy's righthand man, Louie Milito. A couple neighborhood girls even vouched for them as an alibi when the cops showed up.

Studio 54
254 West 54th Street
Manhattan

This legendary hangout opened April 16, 1977, and closed a little more than three years later.

What a glorious three years they were. That's when all the heavy shit started going down: Lufthansa, the Boston College basketball point-shaving scandal. I was going in so many different directions, 54 was more surreal than anything I'd experienced. It had the most beautiful people and some of the craziest shit going on. There was this giant spoon. If you didn't have an ass that could stop a freight train or you weren't connected, you weren't getting in. That's tough to do. I've helped out with lots of joints, and it was always more a mystery how to get people to come in. Studio 54 tried to keep the people out.

The owners were Steve Rubell and Ian Schrager, both New York boys. They were college buddies and had opened some steak houses around town. Steak didn't cut it. Then they bought the old CBS studio on 54th Street. They began to launch history. Rubell partied like a rock star while Schrager was a responsible business wizard. This working relationship had magical results. Studio 54 is the most famous nightclub ever. Everyone who was anyone had to go. It was the place. I wake crying some nights because it's gone. Last I heard, they opened the upper floor for boozing and dancing

Hitting the town, '70s style.

(cleverly named Upstairs Studio 54, 212-445-0190), while the main area is now a high-end theater.

Regine's
Somewhere in New York City

You are not getting the address. Find it yourself. Gotti and other Gambino muscle frequented; you shouldn't.

Mandatory Mob Hangout

Brooklyn House of Detention
Atlanta Avenue
Brooklyn

Every seasoned hood has stopped by here for at least a meal. I don't recommend it: The drinks taste like piss, and the food tastes like shit. Unless you know someone, you'll have quite a few meals. We never went much past the cop station. It was a joke. Someone would call and bam, out. I know Sammy the Bull still had the pull to do that shit. It's no joke these days, though. Take it from me, the joint sucks.

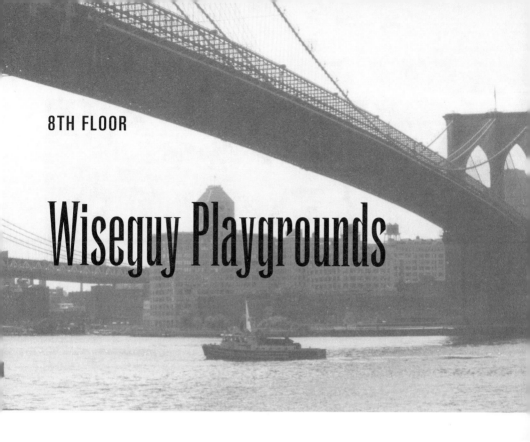

Wiseguy Playgrounds

T ennis players have courts. Golfers have courses. Swimmers
have pools. Gangsters have streets. Crime is the game, and the
streets are the playground.

Hijacking Hotspots

Anytime we needed cash (most days of the week), we could always
count on a hijacking. I don't mean hijacking planes or busloads
full of orphans. I'm talking harmless "rerouting" of merchandise
by the truckload. We'd get the tips from the drivers themselves. After hundreds of these transactions, I don't think I saw one injury,
definitely no shots fired.

The key to successful hijackings is preparation, timing, and location, location, location! There were certain intersections with
multiple routes and favorable law enforcement conditions that
made the late-night jackings a breeze.

Fulton Fish Market. Fresh fish worthy of a king,
or at least a Godfather.

THE AIRPORTS

When most people think of connections at the airport, they think
of making their next flight. We were thinking about making our
next score. Our "connections" were all the relatives and friends we
had that ran the place, from baggage to security, it was a solid
foundation of tips and payoffs. Even as recently as 2002, almost $8
million was heisted out of London Heathrow airport. The airports
were where all the biggest shit went down. It's where the big pay-
days were, and are.

JFK, which in my younger years was called Idlewild Airport,
named after the nearby golf course, was our stomping ground.
When I hear a plane, I wonder if it's a flying jackpot. In 1963, the
airport officially became John F. Kennedy Airport. It's much
tougher to pull shit off nowadays. There are over 200,000 employees, and you would need to know a lot of them to get any kind of
score going. This is where we pulled off the Air France heist. In the

Luftansa heist in 1978, Jimmy the Gent along with Tommy D. and some of the other guys allegedly pulled off the biggest cash burglary in American history, looting $5.8 million from the Lufthansa air cargo terminal.

A different big chunk of waterfront property on Flushing Bay and Bowery Bay in Queens, originally the Gala Amusement Park, became another private flying field in 1929. They began to transform it into a commercial airport in 1937, and by 1939, New York Municipal Airport opened for business. When the Port Authority leased it in 1947, they thankfully changed its name to La Guardia Airport. La Guardia was the government's shining star in the quest to destroy and/or ship out Frank "King of Slots" Costello's enormous slot-machine empire. It's smaller than Kennedy, but in some cases of thievery smaller is better.

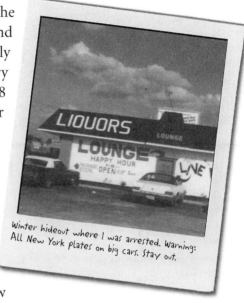

Winter hideout where I was arrested. Warning: All New York plates on big cars. Stay out.

THE DOCKS

The notorious Romano brothers ran the docks in my day. It was a wiseguy waterfront. It was wide open, just like the airport. The docks were controlled by the mob, I don't mean a couple docks here and there, I mean the whole waterfront. During World War II, the government had to go to the mob for help, since they had their pulse on the docks, and the fear of a German U-boat coming into New York harbor was a reality. There was cooperation, a little wheeling and dealing, and there was success in the venture. It eventually got Charles "Lucky" Luciano out of prison, although deported (he was in there on a questionable sentence for prostitution). Goes to show you, when Nazis are involved, we're all on the same team.

The mob's other rackets.

I used to spend a lot of time down there, always scores to be had, and we knew everybody. Even before my time, a lot of those old guys, like Anastasia, were longshoremen. His brother controlled the union. The Mafia had roots down there, a history. If someone crossed them or fucked up, it was easy to get rid of them; I mean you're already at the docks! Who was gonna say anything? I swear I've been down there, and there's always a heavy fishy smell—well sometimes there was another odor, and it wasn't dead fish. We hijacked stuff coming in, and we shipped hijacked stuff out. If we didn't know about a boat or have a piece of it, that boat didn't dock. Of all the hard goods arriving daily, all the riches in the world, we were always looking to score lobster. I think lobsters are responsible for the mob's corruption on the docks.

These days, the mob has really worn out its welcome; they even tried to destroy the old fish market. You may not see many wiseguys now, but they're there. What hasn't changed is the selection of unbelievably fresh fish. All the best city restaurants stampede at dawn to hand-pick the choicest seafood. Fulton Street is the best known and known as the best.

ASTORIA BOULEVARD, QUEENS

Astoria Boulevard was one of the shipping veins between La Guardia and the city. It's also one of the best places in the world to hijack a truck. Just check out the droves of loaded trucks that frequent this freeway-shadowing road. If the loads weren't worth it, we already knew and didn't bother with them. Most times, we knew what was going to be on the truck and then we'd get it even before the shit was loaded on the truck at the airport.

It's unbelievable how many scores came down that boulevard. The easiest goods to move are the simple needs and vices of life. Bigger is tougher to hide. Cigarettes, razor blades, the smaller the stuff, aspirin, stuff that people go through every day, that's what we loved to steal. In my case, liquor and cigarettes. The secret to success is to have the load sold before you hijack it. Just pre-sell the stuff. We always had wholesalers we'd pull right up to. Back in those days it was a lot easier; the trucks didn't even have alarms. Even when the cargo was real valuable stuff, the trucks used to drive out with only a tail car. We'd just nail the tail car first. We didn't care if they had guns. We had bigger guns.

Gangster Trivia

"Swag" is the term for our hijacked inventory. "Shwag" is shitty weed.

The Track

A newspaper reporter in the 1920s heard New Orleans stable hands refer to New York as the "Big Apple." The name stuck and so has the popularity of horse racing, and more important, wagering. There isn't a wagered horse race, in New York or anywhere else, without some kind of mob interaction (or interference).

I was barred from the track for bookmaking when I was sixteen. I was a runner and used to go to the clubhouse a lot. I ran from table to table for this guy Milty. We placed for the Vanderbilts, big money families like that, and all the horse owners and trainers. They bet large sums of money and they didn't want, if the horse was a favorite, to reduce the odds. It spreads like wildfire. If a guy goes up to the window and puts twenty grand to win on a horse, in those days, you could punch only $100 tickets. Long before the guy's finished placing the $20,000 bet, especially if he was a trainer or a horse owner, everybody would jump on that horse, even if it was five-to-two odds; they'd knock it down to even money in a minute. The same shit still goes on to a degree. Back then it was rampant, commonplace, and exciting as hell.

There are plenty of racetracks in the metro New York area where you can place your bets on the horses and win big bucks. Take your pick of tracks, then take your pick of horses. You can't go wrong with the tracks; you may go wrong with the horses. There are various events in horse racing held each year. The largest event is the Belmont Stakes, the third race in the Triple Crown. It is held every spring at Belmont Park.

Aqueduct Race Track
110-00 Rockaway Boulevard
Queens
(718) 641-4700

This is where we made a lot of money; it was right in our backyard, a half mile to the parking lot from Robert's Lounge, and then another half mile across the parking lot. It fits 8,000 cars. This historic track first opened in 1894. Can you imagine how much money has rolled through this joint? The Big A has always been mobbed-up.

Gangster Trivia

In the mob, a loanshark is referred to as "shylock." The interest owed is the "vig." Get behind on the vig, and look the fuck out.

We used to hang out in the backstretch because we weren't allowed on the track. We had a little spot where we could watch the horses with binoculars. We got all the information there, too. They couldn't throw us out of the parking lot, only if we were inside the track. I mean, there were times I got thrown out of the track three, four times a day. They had a special squad called the TRA, a secu-

When at the racetrack, always make it look as if
you're studying the stats and that you haven't been tipped off.

rity squad with pictures of all of us. Then they passed a law where
if they found us in the track, they could get us for trespassing and
prosecute us. It made it a little more difficult.

Belmont Park Racetrack

2150 Hempstead Turnpike
Belmont
(516) 488-6000

Belmont Park is the most beautiful of the local tracks in my opinion. This place not only attracts some of the country's wealthiest
race fans but also has a rich history of its own. Belmont opened in
the spring of 1905. In 1918, the first airmail flight in the country
took off from here and went to D.C. I've always thought it was just
a plane full of mob payoffs for crooked politicians.

Belmont is world famous for the Belmont Stakes, but I love
this place on any race day. It has a longer track than Aqueduct,

which I find more exciting. The track caters to both racing and special events from mid-May to the end of July and then from early September to almost Halloween.

Saratoga Race Track

Union Avenue
Saratoga Springs
(518) 584 6200

This isn't nearby, but it's well worth the drive for a weekend get-away. You are truly up in horse country, and I guarantee this track is older than you. The Saratoga tradition started back in 1863. Aside from being a gorgeous property, Saratoga is the place to take kids if you want to hatch their gambling bug early. In the morning there are free tram rides to the barn areas.

Yonkers Raceway

810 Central Avenue
Yonkers
(914) 968-4200

This is supposed to be the place the Genovese family fixed races for J. Edgar Hoover. In return, J. Edgar denied the existence of the mob. Harness racing is a nice change up, and there's a lot of under-the-radar money to be made. They have year-round racing. Make sure you call, because they used to not race on Sundays or Wednesdays.

Off-Track Betting Corp.

1501 Broadway, 12th Floor
Manhattan
(212) 221-5200; fax: (212) 221-8025
www.nycotb.com

Can't get to the track? Winter? No problem—almost 100 cozy and possible mobster-present branches, with food and wagering. This is where some of the craziest shit goes down. You remove another layer away from the actual track, you add an entire new layer for troublemakers to wedge themselves into. When they smell money, the sharks come swimming.

Cigar Bars

Smoking is one of the mob's pastimes. We were always so damn nervous about getting pinched or hit, we had to smoke. Personally, it took my mind off the reality of my situation. Plus, I was always driving around town, and if you weren't an earner, you were always sitting around. You can't play cards without smoking. You couldn't go to the Copa and refuse a cigar. It just wasn't allowed.

Today in New York they haven't pussed out like the West Coast. You can still smoke in places. Some of the world's best cigar bars north of Cuba. If you play your cards right, you can score some Cubans as well.

Florio's Grill and Cigar Bar
192 Grand Street between Mott and Mulberry Streets
Manhattan
(212) 226-7610

Even if you dislike cigars and smoke, you have to love this spot. It's right out of a mob movie. There are wiseguys and wisegals, a selection of stogies that will blow your lips off, and the unbeatable atmosphere of the Little Italy outskirts.

P/G/Kings
18 West 33rd Street
Manhattan
(212) 290-0080

They don't have the best selection of stogies, but they have a couple good ones. The atmosphere and awesome food make up for the

The junkyards adjacent to Shea Stadium are rumored to be mob-infested.

limited cigar menu. This place has been around over a century. If you're hungry for more than a cigar, eat here, pal.

Belmont Lounge
117 East 15th Street
Manhattan
(212) 533-0009

This is the place the rock stars puff. As you know, mobsters are the rock stars of crime, so you'll find them here as well. It's a great venue with a unique game room. The games are old school classics perfect to play while you smoke. If you don't smoke, don't bother.

Gentlemen's Clubs

Some guys spent more time in these joints than at home. In late 1978, one of the Lucchese soldiers, Franky Cicero, had a lot of pull at a club and ended up actually turning a dressing room into a small apartment/stash pad near the holidays. I swear, it was sick. A half dozen of us had keys made, and during the day we'd be back there with our broads and snorting his coke. Frank got so pissed once when he found his pad "soiled" he went nuts, and the girls had to call the cops. What did he expect?

These joints were perfect for setting up scores. The music was loud, the room was dark, the scenery was great. The strippers were usually nicer and cost less than the wives or girlfriends anyhow. It was all business. A lot of guys didn't have time for drama but still enjoyed seeing some naked women. Plus, where better to butter up a potential business associate than with a cold beer and some hot ass? The girls would always hear about big scores. These drunk dicks would brag to them. We'd get tipped off, they'd get tipped. Strip clubs had it all. There was always shady shit going on you could get a piece of if you wanted. You always paid your lawyer

If you are looking at this sign,
look around; there are mobsters near.

and stripper even before your bookmaker. Chances are there are
wiseguys in every strip joint in New York City every night of the
year. We spent panties full of cash every time we barged in there.
On top of that, if anyone messed with the girls, they came to us
and we took care of it.

Angels
44 Walker Street
Manhattan
(212) 391 0099

Make sure to check what's happening on the night you're hitting
this spot. It's not your typical strip club. Nevertheless, I've had
some great nights here. Worth every penny. Depending on the
night, they might have girls, maybe guys, even guys that look like
girls, and vice versa.

This is where you buy fish
and see the guys that might make you swim with them.

Baby Doll Lounge
34 White Street
Manhattan
(212) 226-4870

They claim this is where Drew Barrymore shed hers. Should have been here that night. Damn it.

Billy's Topless
729 Sixth Avenue
Manhattan

Love this spot. If you're low on dough, this is a great place for eye candy and cheap drinks.

Gaiety Theater
201 West 46th Street
Manhattan
(212) 221-8868

Don't let the name fool you . . . this isn't a movie theater. Yes, it is boys minus their clothes. I've never been in here, but I hear it's nuts. Literally.

Scores

333 East 60th Street
Manhattan
(212) 421-3763

In my experience, it's the best strip club on the planet. It's going to cost you a little, as it should. Rumor has it the Gambinos muscled in here for years and have now been muscled out. Can you blame them? The new one, it's like a whole block, a city. What a beautiful city.

Las Vegas, 2002. Still a mob playground and retreat. I wonder why.

Playing the Numbers

Everybody played the numbers. Housewives, old women, old guys, most of them having nothing to do with the mob other than proximity. It was more of a local unsanctioned lottery than a money scam. It's the last three numbers in the total mutual handle at the racetrack. You could go into the corner of any place and play. Now it's legal. Then it wasn't.

Oh, and Those Other Sports

The mob and sports are attached at the money clip. We watched, manipulated, and bet on all kinds of sports, from chess to hockey.

Madison Square Garden

2 Pennsylvania Plaza at Seventh Avenue
Manhattan
(212) 465-6741

We've run more bets at games that happened here than any other facility in the country. A lot of times you'll see the bookies and gangsters all over the sidewalk at the Seventh Avenue entrance. If you talk to them, make sure you know what you're talking about. Current teams that call "the Garden" home are the New York Knicks, New York Liberty (WNBA), Saint John's Red Storm, and the NHL's New York Rangers.

Yankee Stadium

161st Street and River Avenue
Bronx, NY 10452
(718) 293-4300

I don't think he actually did, but it's called "the house that Ruth built." You haven't lived until you've seen a game here.

Shea Stadium

123-01 Roosevelt Avenue
Flushing, NY 11368
(718) 507-TIXX

This was the first stadium the Beatles ever played in the USA. I missed it. Oh yeah, this is also where the New York Mets play.

Brooklyn Cyclones

On the Boardwalk
Coney Island, Brooklyn
(718) 449-8497

Fitting, since parts of Coney Island look like a cyclone hit them. Just kidding. This is a great place for some good old-fashioned fun.

SPORTS SPOTS YESTERDAY

When I was growing up, the New York Giants played at Yankee Stadium. That was such a great season. Frank Gifford, pre–Kathy Lee, was player of the year, and they took the NFL title. A couple years later was the famous game versus the Colts, where we lost in overtime. I thought we were going to war with Baltimore.

Following suit were the Brooklyn Dodgers who left Ebbets Field in Brooklyn in 1957. That was a shitty year. I remember growing up with the Brooklyn Dodgers. The year that sticks out is

East Harlem in the summer.
Straight out of a mob movie—*The Godfather,* actually.

1955. I was not even ten years old, and it was a magical summer. Brooklyn won the National League pennant and defeated the New York Yankees in the World Series. Lefty pitcher Johnny Podres was the World Series MVP. It was a huge event that ended in Yankee Stadium. I thought there was going to be a civil war between the two boroughs.

NEW YORK MARATHON

If you do a lot of running, other than from the mob, the New York Marathon is in my eyes the best in the world, for spectators and runners. Every year on the second Sunday in November. It's a 26.2-mile run starting in Staten Island at the Verrazano Narrows Bridge Toll Plaza and going through my old hood in Brooklyn. I like to grab a hot dog and watch the crazy fuckers cross the Queensborough (59th Street) Bridge into Manhattan. It's like they just ran into a wall. Then up the East Side to the Bronx, through

Mob turf, Manhattan. Bodies were dumped here, at high tide preferably, so the outgoing tide would suck them out to sea.

the South Bronx, and back into Manhattan. The race finishes in Central Park. Make sure you got a ride back to your car, or learn the subway, pal.

U.S. OPEN TENNIS TOURNAMENT

The mob is full of action and hard hits, as is the U.S. Open at the National Tennis Center in Queens. Annually in late August–early September, including Labor Day weekend.

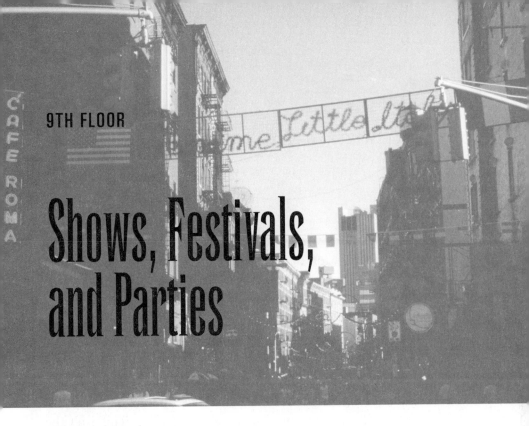

Shows, Festivals, and Parties

New York was the capital of the United States between 1785 and 1790 and in my eyes still is the nation's capital and the world's. There's something for everyone. If you can't find something to do here, you've got problems. There are things happening any time of day or night, any day or night of the year. Many free or inexpensive, and for the fortunate that need to unload some green, you can do it here with unmatched style.

New York has the best theaters and the best shows on the stages. No matter what kind of museum you prefer, New York has many of the best. They shoot some of the world's most popular television shows here, many of which invite spectators. Some of the world's most famous people have been shot here as well. The cemeteries read like the who's who of the who's dead. The city thrives on catering to visitors and does a hell of a job.

Theater

A real New York experience cannot be without the theater. It is the best in the world.

BROADWAY

There's only one Broadway. It's in New York. It's the world's greatest concentration of top theater. Broadway is the best way to seal the deal with the broads. It's the big show, a thespian's and audience's dream. The best things happen when both sides are into it, right?

There's no way "Theater" is mobbed-up? Bullshit. Mobsters love drama, outfits, and staging. Just think about it. Even in the great book, *Donnie Brasco,* Pistone and Woodley explain how some Bonanno guys were planning to stick up the box office of a show they were putting on. Their own box office! This isn't the only story I heard like this. The mob and the performing arts are historically linked. I used to party, and I mean *party* with Sammy Davis Jr. and Frank. They were the best, and they weren't partying with me on some random coincidence.

The theater district runs from 41st Street up to 53rd and is between Ninth Avenue and the Avenue of the Americas.

For tickets and information:

The Broadway Ticket Center
1560 Broadway between 46th and 47th Streets
Manhattan
(888) BROADWAY or call Tele-Charge at (212) 239-6200

OFF-BROADWAY

What's the difference between on and off? One's on, one's not. Who gives a shit. Broadway is so famous, other productions get a piece of the notoriety by being off it.

Dancing and Music Spots

Is there anyone hotter than professional dancers? Not really. Mobsters were always stalking them. If you suck at dancing and have the musical talent of an antelope, here is your chance to see the world's best do their thing.

Carnegie Hall

57th Street at Seventh Avenue
Manhattan
(212) 247-7800

This concert hall has been famous for over 100 years. It's great to catch an orchestra or a nap, depending on your tastes. This place is huge and so are the performers that land gigs. We loved this place. We used to control all the unions that loaded and unloaded (not guns) the instruments for Carnegie. There's a lot of money in that. Every time I see an orchestra on television or advertised in the papers, I think to myself, "Who's taxing that, how many instruments?" We just loved the whole idea of scoring in a hall named after Carnegie. Every powerful criminal in New York has entertained here.

Gangster Trivia

An "empty suit" or "jack-off" was the mobster wanna-be, the guy that just hung around us to feel cool. We were; he wasn't.

Lincoln Center

65th Street and Broadway
Manhattan
(212) 875-5050

Need tix? Call CenterCharge: (212) 721-6500

Lincoln Center is in the middle of the performing arts world. It sports a range of theaters with diverse lineups from great jazz,

Regarding the rumors about me enjoying sausage,
they're half true.

individual performers, to full-scale orchestras. Lincoln Center is
on the West Side, and the unions have always kept it close.

Madison Square Garden

2 Pennsylvania Plaza at Seventh Avenue
Manhattan
(212) 465-6741

Mob built and worked, the Garden was divided up between the
Irish and Italian families and was off to the races. The Garden
takes up two city blocks. The Garden has had the finest of the
finest performers perform there. The best Led Zeppelin shows
ever. You think crazier shit has gone on backstage anywhere else?
No fucking way. On top of that, it's home to the top sports events
the city offers (aside from Yankee games).

Metropolitan Opera House

64th Street where Broadway and Columbus meet
  (part of Lincoln Center)
Manhattan
(212) 362-6000

Even if the closest you've gotten to opera is *Oprah*, you've probably heard of the Metropolitan Opera. It's the grand mansion of
opera houses.

The Joyce Theatre

175 Eighth Avenue at 19th Street
Manhattan
(212) 242-0800

Famed dance theater. If there is a form of dance, it has been or will
be performed here.

Radio City Music Hall

59th Street at Sixth Avenue
Manhattan
(212) 247-4777

If you haven't heard of this landmark, come out of your cave, asshole. It's the most famous music
hall in the world. I used to "date"
a Rockette when I was twenty-five
years old. We'd go right in the
stage door and wait for them.
Paulie's brother Babe, who was a
made guy, he wound up keeping
this chick after we all made her ac-
quaintance. She was beautiful.
What I wouldn't do to go back to
those sessions.

Gangster Trivia

To earn a "button" was to become a made
man, an untouchable.

Brooklyn Academy of Music
30 Lafayette Avenue
Brooklyn
(718) 636-4111

Brooklyn isn't only known for the mob. I've heard that the BAM's vibrant annual slate can hold the attention of even the thickest thug.

Festivals and Feasts

Every neighborhood, especially during the warmer months, has a feast. There are games, music, dancing, and most important, food. All of this is a cheery facade for quick untaxed cash. It's the corruption of these events that makes them so much fun. In my eyes, most parades and festivals are celebrating ways to make money by lightening the padded wallets of masses milling together on the big day.

Feast of San Gennaro
Mullberry Street
Little Italy, Manhattan

San Gennaro is a weeklong celebration in September, one of the most famous in New York, and by far the Italian community's largest event. I used to take that special girl down there. It's magical. They usually hold the feast late summer, after Labor Day. Try the fried calamari, and of course, the sausage and pepper heroes. Every mobster in town will be there.

Not in the too distant past of the late 1990s, the Genovese family made news down at the festival. The boss who stepped in for Gigante, "Barney" Bellomo, was convicted for shaking down the street vendors for a cut of the cash. I would have just asked for a few pounds of heroes. This goes to show you, you show up here, and you'll be in the company of troublemakers.

Columbus Avenue Fair

*Columbus Avenue from 66th to 96th
    Streets*
Manhattan

I have been to this one before. Anything to do with Columbus, you'll find Italians.

Cherry Blossom Festival at Brooklyn Botanic Garden

100 Washington Avenue
Brooklyn
(718) 623-7200

New York's, and the world's, greatest DJ.

Late April. Only in the spring do cherry trees look this nice, so nice some bored wackos decided to have a festival.

Harlem Meer Performance Festival

Lakeside Plaza in Central Park
Manhattan
(212) 860-1370

All Sundays, all summer long. How can you argue with free blues, jazz, and Latin music?

Washington Square Art Exhibit

Bleecker Street to East 12th Street
Greenwich Village, Manhattan
(212) 982-6255

Early summer. This exhibit has been around longer than me, and I guarantee will stay around longer. Over seventy years old. Check out the talent and beauty of New York's art community (and their work).

Film

New York has shitloads of movie theaters from huge cineplexes to tiny arthouses. Wait, if you are visiting NYC and waste two hours on something you can see back home in Omaha, shame on you. I can't argue if you choose to check out one of New York's unique film facilities, however. You can see a bigger variety of movies on a daily basis here than anywhere else in the world. Classic films, foreign films, independent films, even classic foreign independent films, you name it, there's a good chance one is playing right now.

Film Forum

209 West Houston Street
Manhattan
(212) 727-8110

Film Forum, for . . . umm people that appreciate more in film than sex, violence, and rock 'n' roll (not that I'm against those). All kinds of great films at a great movie house. Call and check to see what's playing.

Irish Film Festival at NYU Cantor Center

On campus
Manhattan
(212) 966-3030 x247; Web site: www.filmfleadh.com

We Irish can do more than just get drunk and fight. Every March at least we show you. For schedule details, visit the Web site.

New York Underground Film Festival

Web site: www.nyuff.com

This festival is underground, not underworld. Every March, the NYUFF shocks and succeeds by bringing unusual and usually unseen films to the screen, along with parties.

Walter Reade Theatre
165 West 65th Street
Manhattan
(212) 875-5600

Come to the Reade to watch. That makes sense. They show every type of movie except the type that most people see. There are docs, overseas projects, and films from our homeland projects. As classy as theaters come.

Parades

I'm not a big parade guy, but New York is the parade city. They have parades for shit that most cities might block off a street and sell some funnel cakes. I mean, if you're going to see a parade, it might as well be here. The deep canyon streets, abundant onlookers and participants, and plenty of traffic get fucked up. New York loves parades.

The highlight of my parade season is the eve of the Thanksgiving parade; they inflate the giant balloons around 11 P.M. at the Museum of Natural History by Central Park. You can walk around and check them out. It's pretty cool.

Easter Parade
High 40s through 57th Street along Fifth Avenue
Manhattan

The Italian mob is primarily Catholic, so read between the pews. When the Easter masses let out on Fifth Avenue, crowds of people gather to view the parade. It's a great way to spend a Sunday in spring, even if you're Jewish or Satanic.

St. Patrick's Day Parade
Fifth Avenue from 44th to 86th Streets and then to Third Avenue
Manhattan

On or around St. Paddy's Day and second only to the parade in Chicago. They won't have their own float, but keep an eye out for

A few people wandered out for a summer festival.

the Irish mobsters. All are present on this payday. The legendary binge turns 250 years old in 2011. That's a lot of drinking over the years. This should be on the top of your parade hit list if you like drinking as much as parading. I have never been here sober. Has anyone?

Greek Independence Day Parade
Fifth Avenue from 62nd to 79th Streets
Manhattan

Around Easter and well worth it for the number of stunning Greek broads. The Greek mob is not one to fuck with, so a lot of guys come here to show their support. Personally, I support Greek women. They are mesmerizing.

Salute to Israel Parade

Fifth Avenue from 57th to 79th Streets, then east to Third Avenue
Manhattan
(212) 245-8200 x255

Early May. I'm half Jewish, so I try to make it every other year. Can you guess what the theme of this spring parade is? NYPD worked overtime at this one in 2002, an understatement.

Gangster Trivia

Sit-downs were our version of court. They were held in basements and back rooms of restaurants or social clubs. We settled disputes at these meetings including those involved and the respective family heads.

Norwegian-American Parade

90th Street and Fifth Avenue, north
on Fifth Avenue to 67th Street
and Seventh Avenue
Bay Ridge, Brooklyn
(718) 761-8815

The seventeenth of May. There is plenty to see at this one, but this should be more than reason enough to attend: the crowning of Miss Norway. If you are a man, even a gay man, and you come here, you'll fall in love. P-u-l-ease.

Thanksgiving Day Parade

Starts at Columbus Circle and goes over two miles down Fifth
Avenue to 34th Street, ending at Macy's of all places
Manhattan

Historically sponsored by Macy's. As I mentioned earlier, I prefer the night prior. Every year, Dave "Wally" Ironsini dressed up like a pilgrim carrying a whiffle ball bat. He was a hell of a player, a tough old bird from Tom's River, New Jersey, and had the attitude of a pissy cougar. He tried to knock as many guys in the butt as he could. Needless to say, he got his own ass kicked annually.

Museums

To me, the entire city is a museum—the history and architecture, the crazy shit that's gone down here. If I weren't such a bullet magnet, I'd love to wander and explore the boroughs.

Unlike most art lovers, we wiseguys checked out museums only to see if we could rip them off. I'd be standing there next to a couple of uptown yo-yos, and they're thinking, "Oh, this is a beautiful piece from the French Revolution." I'm thinking, "How much is this ugly piece of shit worth, who can move it for me, and how the fuck do I get it out of here?" This is called checking the heist potential. Back then, some jobs were cake, some only for you Thomas Crown–like fuckers. The best way in was to pay off some sap making four dollars an hour to protect $400 million in art. Tens of thousands of pieces of art are stolen annually. See what I mean? These guys want to screw those rich fucks and get a little themselves. Nowadays computers are tougher to bribe, so you must remember this rule: The more expensive the item, the tighter the security system.

If you're into museums proper, you go to Manhattan. It's tough to hit all the gems between 70th and 105th Streets, but like me, almost worth taking a shot at.

American Craft Museum
40 West 53rd Street
Manhattan
(212) 956-3535

If you're in the mob and caught fiddling with crafts, it's certain death. Now that I'm out, I can enjoy the surprisingly interesting exhibits. Great place to take a gal that's really into basket weaving and shit like that. I'm kidding; drop her.

Heist potential: Who gives a shit about crafts? Not much value on the craft fair black market.

Brooklyn Museum of Art
200 Eastern Parkway
Brooklyn
(718) 638-5000

This is almost the largest art museum in the city, and I think the best. Always good shit to see here. I'm not just saying so because I'm from Brooklyn.

Heist potential: Oh boy, some worthy items, but the security staff gets tipped more than waiters. Too close to home.

Cooper-Hewitt National Design Museum
2 East 91st Street
Manhattan
(212) 849-8400

The CH is the Big Apple's franchise branch of the Smithsonian Institution. It's a good excuse at the least to go visit a mansion built by Carnegie.

Heist potential: The property itself is sweet but wouldn't be my choice for scores, not enough retirement pieces.

El Museo del Barrio
1230 Fifth Avenue at 104th Street
Manhattan
(212) 831-7272

Does the name give it away? This welcoming museum displays works by Latin American artists. There is some amazing stuff to be viewed here. Located in the heart of Spanish Harlem.

Heist potential: This isn't the tourist shit you find coming back from Tijuana. There are some beautiful pieces in here, and more important, some are rare and priceless.

Fraunces Tavern Museum
54 Pearl Street
Manhattan
(212) 425-1778

This is where George Washington would have had sit-downs if there were any beefs during the Revolutionary War. They probably cracked a lot of crude redcoat jokes.

Heist potential: This is mostly American history only a few hundred years old and deals with us. What's that mean? Don't bother. Most definitely worth a social visit, though.

Frick Collection
1 70th Street
Manhattan
(212) 288-0700

Henry Clay Frick's mansion displaying his collection of more than 500 years worth of great art.

Heist potential: This could be a fun one, but you'd need to pull off some *Great Muppet Caper* shit. This place is bulging with dollar signs.

Intrepid Sea-Air-Space Museum
46th Street and 12th Avenue
Manhattan
(212) 245-0072

They left nothing out of the title for this one. It's actually on a huge aircraft carrier docked on the Hudson.

Heist potential: Unless you can steal the whole ship, just enjoy it for the history and technology.

Typical New York alleged mob-related wedding surveillance photo.

The Metropolitan Museum of Art
1000 Fifth Avenue
Manhattan
(212) 535-7710

They told me there are many millions worth of priceless ancient artwork and artifacts. We dreamed of robbing this spot, but the security staff could not be bribed past the grand entrance.

Heist potential: This is the one. Get your best expert operatives, do years of planning, hope for loads of luck, and you might be able to swipe some treasures from this crown jewel of art museums. The ultimate caper.

Museum of the City of New York
Fifth Avenue at 103rd Street
Manhattan
(212) 534-1672

You guessed right. This museum deals with the city itself and its people. You can learn more about New York's history and future here in one day than you can prancing around town for weeks. Packed with fascinating local history, and there's plenty of it.

Heist potential: I'd say if you're gonna rob a city's history, go down to Philly.

Museum of Jewish Heritage—A Living Memorial to the Holocaust
18 First Place
Battery Park City
New York
(212) 509-6130

Having a bad day? A quick stop here, you'll reevaluate your priorities. If this doesn't give you perspective, you should be a murderer for the Mafia, I could make some calls for you.

Heist potential: Not that kind of museum.

National Academy Museum and School of Fine Arts
1083 5th Avenue at 89th Street
Manhattan
(212) 369-4880

American art, so you won't find anything too ancient.

Heist potential: Some of this stuff is great but won't raise the eyebrows of illegal buyers high enough.

Scandanavia House: The Nordic Center in America
58 Park Avenue
Manhattan
(212) 779-3587

Their art, like their women, is quite beautiful.

Heist potential: Why risk pissing off Scandanavian women?

Solomon R. Guggenheim Museum
Fifth Avenue at 89th Street
Manhattan
(212) 423-3500

A must-visit for anybody. The art is topnotch, but the building it-self is the strangest I've ever visited. Tons of ladies, too. Get stoned before you arrive at this spiral curiosity. Frank Lloyd Wright did nothing wrong designing this uptown landmark.

Heist potential: I fucking dare you.

Art Galleries

Trying to make some uptown girl think you're intellectual? Trying to score some free wine and cheese? Do you have too much time on your hands? Too much money? Are you planning on robbing an art gallery and selling the works on the black market? If you answered yes to any of these questions, this may be your scene. New York is full of art galleries stocked with some of the world's greatest (and most expensive) art. At the same time, in the same city, SoHo streets offer amazing art at street prices. Either way, if you're into art at all, you came to the right place.

Animazing Gallery
474 Broome Street
Manhattan
(212) 226-7374

Lives up to its name. A little jaunt off the typical art form trail.

Leo Castelli

59 East 79th Street
Manhattan
(212) 249-4470

Sounds like a mob joint, but actually one of the finest collections of art to ever enter SoHo (he was one of the first).

CFM Gallery

112 Greene Street
SoHo, Manhattan
(212) 966-3864

If a building was "one of ours" it was union built and run during our rule. We controlled it.

Not sure what CFM stands for, could be Can't Find (enough) Money. This place always has impressive shows and often has pieces by well-known artists like Dali.

Rehs Gallery

5 East 57th Street
Manhattan
(212) 355-5710

All this stuff is older than you, and some of it's worth more, too. Always worth stopping by when you're in town.

Where to Go If You Get Shot

If you happen to get shot at a parade or after a heist, it is important to know where to go. Just like the movies, we had doctors on the payroll. It was a 24/7 housecall stab-and-gunshot-wound service. We'd have surgery in the kitchens of our restaurants, on card tables, wherever we ended up. We stayed the fuck away from hospitals. They equal trouble. This one guy, Dr. Muncy, was so in debt for gambling, he was like our crew's personal physician. If you don't have this luxury, there are a few places I recommend that can really tend to your fresh holes. Getting in some heat in the hospital is better than dying.

Albert Einstein-Weiler Hospital
1825 Eastchester Road
Bronx
(718) 904-2000

Cabrini Medical Center
227 East 19th Street
Manhattan
(212) 995-6658

Other great places for low-key patch ups are the local universities. Columbia uptown and NYU midtown are two of the best medical programs in the world. I met these kids, Josh and Nancy, both good-looking med students, in 2001 at a bar on the Lower East Side. We got to drinking, and I mentioned my ex-association with med students in the 1970s. They admitted they were approached the prior year by a couple of mob punks. A third was lying in the back seat of the car. A lot of money flashed. They ran. It happened right outside their hall at NYU (How-ston, asshole) at about 3 A.M. on a Wednesday, after they were catching up on late night work. Same shit, different decade.

Shopping and Shoplifting

Paying the Mob Tax

The mob taxes truckloads of products and services every day. This is not some tax that appears on the receipt as "Mob Tax Percentage." Oh no. This is a tax hidden deep in the item itself and matches or exceeds the other crook's, I mean the government's, piece. The mob can't survive on big scores alone. By involving itself in a variety of steps from production to retail, it carves out slices here and there along the way.

PIPING AND WIRING

One of my favorite pastimes is laying pipe. That said, I'll tell you how we got in on so much of the plumbing and electricity in New York. Stemming from the already lucrative construction rackets, building supplies are the next in a line of wallet-wideners. Piping doesn't go in a house won on a mob bid unless a mob associate provides the pipes, meaning the mob gets a piece of the job. A set-up fee so to speak.

The mob's reach goes even beyond new buildings. I knew a guy, Richie "Rosy" Marino, a low, low worker bee for the Colombo association with rosy cheeks. Instead of construction, he was into destruction. When they would get into any new areas, Richie would whack, snip, and drill through wires and pipes until the locals were begging for new product. So the "affiliated" plumbers and electricians got all this work from one guy's rampage. Once you got it fixed by a connected contractor, which Richie got a piece of, which his higher-ups also got a piece of, you were fine. No problems with the plumbing or electricity, that is until Richie, or someone above him, had a bad day at the track and started whacking again.

CEMENT AND ASPHALT

How could a city with so many foundations and sidewalks not catch the eye of ambitious wiseguys back at the turn of the century? Even in the 1940s, we had dirt walks and streets in parts of Brooklyn. That old cobblestone was for the birds, although the mob controlled the shipping and placing of that, too. You have all this building going on with one common ingredient: cement. If anyone tried to fill anything more than a crack in the sidewalk without us, they got a crack in their skull. From the making to the mixing to the laying, we had it all. There's not a building in the city today that doesn't have a layer of pure Mafia cement.

CLOTHING

The garment center in Manhattan was a mob nest. We controlled it. You couldn't get a sewing machine needle without going through us. If we saw dresses we liked, we made sure they never made it back onto the truck. If I needed a new suit or pajamas, I could swing through and snag them. No one was going to say anything, because everyone working there was there because we said so. Besides, everyone made out anyhow. It was the consumers and retailers who picked up the tab.

I used to grab dresses from this guy, Marco Ripps. He always parked in a white van near the corner of 3rd and Avenue B in Alphabet City. They were some of the best dresses I ever laid eyes on. Who knows where he got them? If Marco's still there, tell him hello for me.

Wiseguy fashion at its peak.

GAME TICKETS

Forget Ticketmaster. What about Union-master, the Mafia? Most places in New York, from the guy that rips your ticket when you enter the game all the way along to the guy that cleans up your puke in the bathroom after the game, are union, and different ones at that. The mob-controlled unions open up the arenas and then work them. They jack up ticket prices like they'll jack up a city official who complains. Keep your mouth shut and enjoy the game.

JEWELRY

All the jewelers from the street vendors outside Penn Station to the boutiques on Fifth Avenue had to get permission from the mob. Can't say it works exactly like this today, but I'll tell you what, in the old days you couldn't sell a cufflink without paying a tribute. The trick was finding new ways to keep jewelry from getting to the shelves easily. On top of that, jewelers paid us just not to rob them. The jeweler Mickey Rubenstein had a setup down the road from me on Queens Boulevard. He had the in on all the shipments. He'd tip us off. What did he get out of it? We didn't rob him, and we didn't kill him.

I have a few favorite jewelry stores in the city.

Wempe
700 Fifth Avenue at 55th Street
Manhattan
(212) 397-9000

They have the pulse on the jewelry world.

Louis Martin Jewelers
54 West 50th Street between Fifth Avenue and the Avenue of the
*　　Americas (Rockefeller Plaza)*
Manhattan

You can get the famous city souvenir charms here. They also have items for those with a larger budget.

Jaded
1048 Madison Avenue
Manhattan
(212) 288-6631

If you are dating someone a little off the beaten trail, this is the renowned place to get away from traditional jewelry.

BOOZE

Wonder why beers are five bucks a glass at dive bars? It's not only the rent. Refusing to release its grasp on the grand days of Prohibition, the mob kept its hold on the majority of the again-legal liquor trade. Bootleggers became important importers, the underground bar owners became licensed liquor vendors, and everyone kept the profits coming. The fact remains, not just anyone can import booze, not just anyone can sell it. That's how it was in Prohibition. The difference being then it was just "no." Now it's "yes, but, and but this and that." It's a fucking lark.

　　There is a mob-style scam that's flooded the livers of wiseguys for decades and probably still does. You get together a crew of riffraffers that owe you a favor. They come in and bust up a joint for a few nights. You show your face and try to help out. Then you approach the owner with an offer of help. Yes, you're gonna help them clean the place up. Say, "Hey, I know who these guys run with and I know someone that could put a stop to this, quietly." Believe me, once you say this, they'll be begging you for help. Now, just as long as they pay their dues to your boss, the troublemakers disappear, and you have a bottomless tab. This happened all the time, and there was nothing anyone could do about it.

Mobster Shopping Methods

If we wanted something, we just stole it. In the rare case we couldn't steal it outright, the currency of choice was U.S. cash, preferably counterfeit, or stolen credit cards, preferably AMEX. There used to be a lot of dummy cash floating around New York in the 1960s and 1970s. One ring got pinched after a punk Benjie was used at a popular (especially with the politicians and wiseguys) massage parlor in downtown Manhattan. When one of the girls brought the deposit to the bank, the fake hundred was flagged, and since there was surveillance on the joint, the cops narrowed it down to a couple questionables from the West Side. The rule was not to use the counties unless: 1) It was somewhere no one knew your face, in other words, outside the city; or 2) It was at least somewhere you knew law enforcement wasn't snapping surveillance photos of you. This wiseguy knew this, but when you're sore, I guess you'll do anything for a good massage.

Thieves invented credit cards, I'm sure of it. When Mastercard and Visa were in that window of time between non-secure usage and growing credit lines and store acceptance, it was a magical era. It was a time of joy and happiness coming in the form of Sunday afternoon Fifth Avenue shopping sprees. Then there were the huge nights on the town with bottomless bar tabs and topless women. I'm talking huge nights. If I wasn't at the diner with my buddies at 9 A.M. after just dropping some broads off, comparing notes of our exploits, it wasn't a good night. I had few bad ones.

Drugs

Drugs and the mob are attached at the hip. Under the counter, over the counter, and off of the counter, we did them all. It was the way most of the guys dealt with the stress, with the fact of membership for life, and to mellow out their wives. As much as the families claimed to be opposed to the drug trade, it has been and is a cash cow for organized crime. They can't resist. I mean it's not like selling retail items that have long lives. Cars, for instance, keep for years. Drugs go out of your hands, into their nose, vein, or mouth, and bam, they're gone, and the customer is back for more. Plus, you're selling an addiction. Believe me, I know—the more the customer does, the more they want. No pun intended, but it snowballs. You lose the business only when a fuck ODs or goes clean, usually the former.

Gangster Trivia

The Gambinos rocked Wall Street in 2001 with a signature "inflate and skate" scam. Stefi Graf supposedly lost hundreds of thousands in a matter of months.

If you are dumb enough to be looking for the hard stuff and don't have any connections, try a cab driver. After I landed in 2002, my cabbie from an area airport offered me assistance in scoring some crack up in Spanish Harlem, not that I took him up on it. No way. Speaking from my multiple experiences, stay clean while in the city; it's a more productive trip. Danger finds you quicker when you're whacked out.

LEGIT DRUGSTORES

It is so easy to get sick in New York. I didn't say sick of New York. The germs run rampant. Be especially careful holding subway poles and rubbing your eyes, flushing toilets, sucking your thumb, and breathing on the congested sidewalks. If you do get sick in the city, the following are a collection of the best pharmacies around.

Fulton Street Pharmacy
1413 Fulton Street
Brooklyn
(718) 638-5088

Ansonia Pharmacy
442 Avenue of the Americas
Manhattan
(212) 477-0762

There's always something available here. It's amazing how spun you can get without a prescription. Lots of powerful folks trust their pill intake to this great pharmacy.

Canarsie Plaza Pharmacy
8707 Flatlands Avenue
Brooklyn
(718) 257-2344

You can often score on other parts of this street without entering a store. (Hint: Head toward the water.) If you're playing it safe or for heaven's sake actually ill, this is one of the best full-service pharmacies around.

Guns

Guns aren't just for whacking anymore. When I was growing up, a pistol was to a mobster what a sword is to a Samurai. Guns were all over the place. Everyone had loaded heat stashed in homes, cars, and on the body at all times. I mean even my shitter had a .38 taped behind the porcelain. My favorite was a .32 Berretta. New York's gun shops have some of the finest offerings of today's gun makers. In my thirty years in the mob, I never once bought a gun that had a warranty, but I don't recommend the black market. Whether you prefer a 9mm semiautomatic, a .44 magnum rifle, a .38 Smith & Wesson, a Walther PPK .380, or a Ruger .357, all mob favorites, New York has places to get them. If we did buy guns from a store, we'd always have to lose them after something went down. If not, the law can trace the bullets or gun back to you. It's much better to have the cops trace them to the poor shit that had his piece stolen from him. Melting them down was the surefire way to clean yourself of a crime. That being said, we were frequent customers.

Perry's Gun Shop
9402 Fort Hamilton Parkway
Brooklyn
(718) 833-1199

Shooters & Anglers Sport Shop
6105 Grand Avenue
Flushing, Queens
(718) 894-6122

Bay Ridge Rod & Gun Club Inc.
6718 Fort Hamilton Parkway
Brooklyn
(718) 745-1067

Burial Accessories (Nontraditional)

Tools of the trade include shovels, saws, hatchets, cement, and razors. Don't forget plenty of gloves and sturdy bags for the body parts. This line of work gets a little messy at times. Digging graves equals blisters. All these items and more can be found at neighborhood hardware stores.

Ace Hardware
130 Fourth Avenue
Manhattan
(212) 673-4292

Ace is the place if you need to bury a corpse in a race.

Angelo's Hardware Store
579 Sutter Avenue
Brooklyn
(718) 346-0479

Conveniently located in Brooklyn not far from a lot of unmarked graves. I heard Bay Ridge tough guy, Manny Russo, a dangerous combo of balls and stupidity, returned a shovel the next day, saying, "This piece of shit took us all night to dig one fucking grave." Doubt this is true, but the kid who told me swears by it.

Benn's Hardware Store
4229 Bell Boulevard
Flushing, Queens
(718) 229-1239

Tony's Hardware Store
181 Smith Street
Brooklyn
(718) 596-9663

Funerals

In the mob, funerals are as much social events as they are farewells. They are attended by as many enemies as friends, loved ones as hated ones, real family and "extended" family. In June of 2002, the Dapper Don was buried in the family mausoleum at St. John's Cemetery in Queens, next to his son. The service took place at Papavero Funeral Home (7227 Grand Avenue, Flushing, 718-651-3535) and had Cuban-cigar and poker-hand floral arrangements. The crowd was a who's who of

Gangster Trivia

Ed McDonald, the U.S. Attorney who took my ass into the Witness Protection Program and had a big hand in taking down Gotti, actually played himself in Goodfellas. The Bonnano family, accused of trying to inflate the New York Post circulation through its foreman in 1992, are also accused of his death.

the who's crooked. The Catholic bishop denied the Gotti family a Christian burial service. Why? Hmmm, I wonder. Probably because John Gotti was what he was.

Goumada Shopping

In the mob, furs were popular heist items. A rack of furs was a rack of forgiveness from our disgruntled female companions.

Fur and Furgery
208 West 29th Street
Manhattan
(212) 244-7601

Herds of furs, real and synthetic, to please those classy ladies.

Henry Cowit, Inc.
151 West 29th Street
Manhattan
(212) 594-5824

I remember when a trip to this store was a ticket out of trouble. Ladies don't seem to dig furs like they used to, but you never know.

No matter what, if there is ever a fix-all to all problems or disagreements with your broad, buddy, goumada, or girlfriend, it is shopping. It's the only proven cure for bitch-itus. Take her shopping and all is forgiven. Take her shopping, and you are getting lucky tonight, or even this afternoon. Just take her shopping, and she's yours. New York has some of the best shopping, and if you know where to go, you can do it without breaking the bank. If you know where to go, you'll buy more than clothes and jewelry. You'll buy yourself another week or two of peace and quiet. You can't put a price on that, my friend.

Goumada Shopping Key

$ = a steal
$$ = the broad is really cute
$$$ = the bitch must be blackmailing you

UPTOWN

Addison on Madison $
698 Madison Avenue between 62nd and 63rd Streets
(212) 308-2660

Good selection of offbeat designs and designers. The price is right. You can't go wrong.

Billy Martin's $
220 East 60th Street between Second and Third Avenues
(212) 861-3100

Wanna shake things up a bit, partner? Trying to impress a recent foxy Texas transplant? This is the place. From cowboy boots to belt buckles, Billy Martin's is a nice detour off the main trail. You'll be knocking boots in no time.

Club Monaco $
1111 Third Avenue at 65th Street
(212) 355-2949

Low prices, high quality. Casually dressy.

Prada $ $ $
4200 841 Madison Avenue at
  70th Street
(212) 327-4200

Trendy, famous label designer clothes for the fast crowd with fat wallets. For very hip chicks with very slender hips.

Gangster Trivia

Marty allowed my real daughter to be one of the "Marias" in the wedding scene of Goodfellas. This was a huge secret on the set due to the hit still on my family.

Big Drop $ $
1321 Third Avenue between 75th and 76th Streets
(212) 988-3344

On the edge of the fashion world.

MIDTOWN

Saks Fifth Avenue $ $ $
611 Fifth Avenue
(212) 753-4000

Yes, it's the department store that made Fifth Avenue famous. Known for its size, selection, location, high prices, and attentive staff.

Banana Republic $ $
656 Fifth Avenue at 50th Street
(212) 974-2350

No, I'm not kidding. Hit the bottom floor of the Rockefeller Center flagship and score on some simple and stylish costumes. You'll still have money in your pocket to buy drinks for the girl you meet upstairs.

Henri Bendel $ $ $
712 Fifth Avenue between 55th and 56th Streets
(212) 247-1100

If you want to lose her for a while, drop by this place. Not only do women love the selection, but there are a lot of walls and hallways to get rid of her in.

Stuart Weitzman $ $
625 Madison Avenue between 58th and 59th Streets
(212) 750-2555

Buy her a couple pairs of footwear here, and she won't be kicking you out of bed for quite some time.

Searle $ $ $
609 Madison Avenue between 57th and 58th Streets
(212) 753-9021

Hot and good-looking (hopefully much like your goumada) lines of women's clothing and sportswear.

SOHO AND THE VILLAGE

Catherine Malandrino $ $ $
468 Broome Street at Greene
(212) 925-6765

Models flood this hot store, so I love it. They have a great sensibility for fashion, so I hear.

Oasis $ $
138 Spring Street at Wooster
(212) 219-0710

This is an oasis for the eye, not for the wallet.

Victoria's Secret $ $
155 Fifth Avenue
(212) 477-4118

Shopping here will make it no secret what you're looking forward to. Please *do not* miss a visit with your loved (or just lovely) one. Prices are great, and the product even better.

For Yourself, Wiseguy

Good suits and wiseguys are joined at the hip. In my day, for a night on the town, if you weren't wearing at least a $1,000 suit, you were treated like a $10 whore. I mean, we weren't the most fashion sensible, I realize. We wore a lot of cheesy stuff, but our suits were slick. I mean, the Italians know

Gangster Trivia

"Junkyard dogs" are connected guys in scrapyards.

their suits. We got them a little differently than the average shopper. We knew guys at the distributors, and we knew which trucks were shipping which sizes. We knew the good stores, and we'd get the trucks before they got there. We'd have meat lockers and pantries of our restaurants filled with racks of suits, because our closets at home were full.

Wiseguy Shopping Key

$ = this will get you decent at a more than decent price

$ $ = you have a solid bank account and taste in threads

$ $ $ = can I get in on some of that action?

Barneys New York $ $

575 Fifth Avenue, Floor 11
Manhattan
(212) 450-8300

Go to the third floor and don't leave until you've found the suit of your dreams. You won't be there long.

Bergdorf Goodman: The Men's Store $ $ $

745 Fifth Avenue at 58th Street
Manhattan
(212) 753-7300

The top designers put their best here, including Armani. You need a fat wallet and a full day, but this is the upper echelon of men's shopping. New York's elite shop here. Hey, they were our favorite people to steal from.

Designer Menswear $ $

598 Broadway at Houston Street
Manhattan
(212) 966-1213

Designer Menswear has a great selection of Armani and Boss, among others. You can trust these guys, even when they measure your inseam. They cater well to big guys, too. The Mafia has no shortage of big waistlines.

Frank Stella $ $
921 Seventh Avenue at 58th Street
Manhattan
(212) 957-1600

Frank Stella looks great, I bet. Lots of guys swear by his selections and deals. Plus, this is one of my favorite neighborhoods in town. Tons of ladies strolling around, so shop here in the spring.

Ermenegildo Zegna $ $ $
743 Fifth Avenue between 57th and 58th Streets
Manhattan
(212) 421-4488

Some of the best ties in the world, too expensive and nice for bloodstains, and strong enough to choke your enemy.

INA Men $ $
262 Mott Street between Houston and Prince Streets
Manhattan

You wouldn't know this place is a secondhand store. It's a good spot if you're running low on cash but need to look good.

Time for a Real Watch

New York has the widest selection of knock-off street vendor watches in the country. It also has some of the classiest timepiece selections in the world. If you are in the market for a Rolex, head to:

Plaza Watch & Jewelry Exchange
145 West 57th Street
Manhattan
(800) 772-0054

Staying In

S taying in? You suck.

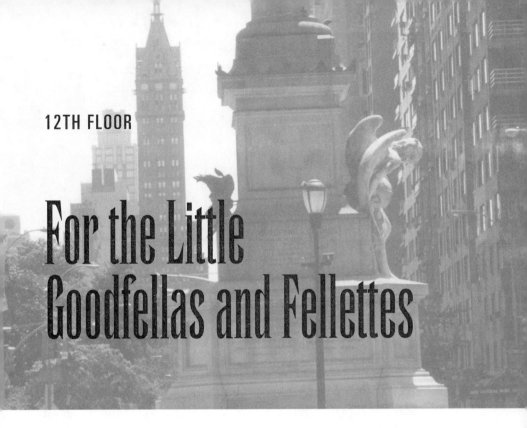

For the Little Goodfellas and Fellettes

New York is no Disneyland. Kids leave Disney singing, "It's a small world after all," but they may leave the city crying, "It's a big scary world after all." New York is a playground but one built for adults. My advice, leave the little goodfellas and fellettes home. You and they are better off. Believe me, I know this may not be an option, so here are some things I found to make the whole experience better.

Leaving them in the room? Elite Nannies (1-866-ELITE44) are rumored to be the elite of the nannies. They'll come to your hotel and keep your kids safe and sound while you hit the town and get into trouble.

Kids' Grub

EJ's Luncheonette
447 Amsterdam Avenue
Manhattan
(212) 873-3344

I swear kids built this place with their own in mind. Top-notch peanut butter and jelly along with dinosaur-shaped chicken nuggets, probably payable with your kids' allowance.

Mars 2112
Broadway at 51st Street
Manhattan
(212) 582-2112

Whether your kids love aliens or just look like them, this is the theme restaurant you actually take a spaceship to get to, or at least that's what they try to trick your children into believing. Great fun, great food, all without even digging into the child support.

Serendipity
225 East 60th Street
Manhattan
(212) 838-3531

The ice cream is so good at the famous Serendipity. I propose children from all around the world deserve one bite. It's that good. They're not shy on the portions either. Definitely not just a creamery, there's tasty and friendly food, too, but the ice cream is what it's famous for.

BEST BURGERS

New York has the best of many things, including burgers. Nothing makes kids, or me, happier than a perfect burger and fries. I mentioned Molly's Irish Pub at 287 Third Avenue in chapter 2. Their burger is nothing to joke about, and I highly recommend it. Here are a couple other grill and charbroil perfectionists the kids will flip over.

Wollensky's Grill
205 East 49th Street
Manhattan
(212) 753-0444

The burgers are juicy on this sandwich side of the famous steak house. If burgers aren't your thing, there are plenty of alternative winners, including the creamed spinach. I swear there are a couple ex-mobsters that work here.

J.G. Melon
1291 Third Avenue
Manhattan
(212) 744-0585

The burgers and old tavern atmosphere are both as good as they get. There are good old American beers on tap for the adults, as well as one of the city carnivore's favorite burgers. I'm not a huge fan of the fries but don't let my opinion stop you.

Shopping

At most stores, kids just whine about not getting anything. In New York, some of the stores are so impressive and fun your kids may forget about the whole buying process. Probably not, but it's worth a shot.

The Disney Store
711 Fifth Avenue at 55th Street
Manhattan
(212) 749-8390

This has to be the biggest Disney store. It's almost an amusement park. Keep an eye on them, your kids could get lost in here, or take them here if you want to lose them.

Corrupted Youth. That's me.

FAO Schwarz
767 Fifth Avenue at 58th Street
Manhattan
(212) 644-9400

This is the store that inspired the famous piano scene in the film *Big*. It has every kind of toy imaginable and then some. The best, or worst, part about this place is the kids can play with the toys.

Toys 'R Us Times Square
1514 Broadway
Manhattan

This place is bigger than most kids' imaginations. There's a Ferris wheel they can ride and giant dinosaur robots roaming the store. They had none of this shit when I was a kid, damn it.

The NBA Store
666 Fifth Avenue at 52nd Street
Manhattan
(212) 515-6221

Like many of my old associates, this place has a lot of balls. Whether your kids need some NBA jerseys and mugs or just need to work on their jump shot, this is the store.

The NBC Experience Store
30 Rockefeller Center Plaza
Manhattan
(212) 664-3700

This is one of those rare stores kids flip for and never forget. With all the Muppet-like cast of NBC's news and talk shows, they have an array of personalized interactive items for sale. You can also purchase anything under the sun bearing the peacock logo. There is also a studio tour available that goes behind the scenes of many shows.

The Scholastic Store

557 Broadway between Prince and Spring Streets
Manhattan
(212) 343 6166

Scholastic is the brand that successfully makes learning bearable. Since I never graduated from high school, I should be in here more than I am. For kids of all ages, this SoHo schooling shop has much more than just books.

Museums

Museums are usually the last thing a kid wants to go see, unless your kid is a nerd. New York has some youngster-friendly places that you might even enjoy.

Chelsea Pier Sports Complex

On the Hudson River/Westside
*   Parkway between 18th and 23rd*
*   Streets*
Manhattan

Gangster Trivia

The very newspapers that boast the mob busts are delivered via the Newspaper and Mail Deliverers Union, the subject of extensive criminal investigation.

This gigantic complex is a treat. You can play almost every imaginable sport here, indoors. It has a couple full-sized turf fields, batting cages, a climbing wall, and then some. The famous driving range is more sophisticated than most on Wall Street. If you can find a way to skate, this spot has a rink for you. They also house the studio for *Law and Order*. Not my kind of show.

Gangster Trivia

Gotti Jr. chose to build his late '90s home fortress in an exclusive area of Oyster Bay Cove, Long Island.

Children's Museum of Manhattan
212 West 83rd Street between Broadway and Amsterdam Avenue Manhattan
(212) 721-1234

I am so pissed they don't have museums like these for adults. This place kicks ass. Its exhibits are separated into age groups, so as your kids visit through the years, they don't have to do the same things every time. There's a Dr. Seuss interactive area. For kids a little more mature, like six years old, there's a working media setup they can shoot, edit, and watch each other on a television show. When I was growing up, I thought a place was a children's museum if it had a fucking gumball machine.

Ellis Island
Via Ferry from Battery Park
Manhattan
(212) 363-3200

Your kids may not appreciate Ellis Island the day they see it, but it's a great experience they'll remember. Almost 20 million immigrants came through this building that's now a museum. Kids always like boat rides, anyhow.

Madame Tussaud's New York
234 West 42nd Street
Manhattan
(800) 246-8872

This is not a whorehouse. As real as wax figures get, this monstrous museum boasts hundreds of celebrities, many in the vein of New York City.

Rose Center
Central Park West at 81st Street
Manhattan
(212) 769-5100

The most entertaining types of museums are ones with a huge planetarium complex. Rose Center is one of the best in the galaxy.

The New York Hall of Science
111th Street and 48th Avenue
Flushing Meadows, Corona Park, Queens
(718) 699-0005

This is the perfect blend of education, fun, and low cost. There are lots of games, all with valuable lessons, so you kill three birds with one stone. It's not in Manhattan but neither are the Yankees.

The youngsters take part in hands-on activities and will learn about kinetic energy, angular momentum, and simple machines. There's this huge seesaw in the science-oriented playground that balances a whole classroom of kids together. I'm serious. There are actually "natural" games that even raised my eyebrows. I didn't grow up with Playstation or even Atari. Nice to see the youngsters here getting away from the television.

Neat Places Kids Love

New York Botanical Garden
Bronx River Parkway at Fordham Road
Bronx
(718) 817-8700

You may see mobsters here today. We used to come here for important discussions. The garden is big and beautiful, no one can hear you, and it smells nice. What more could a mobster want for a quiet talk?

New York Aquarium
Surf Avenue and West 8th Street
Brooklyn
(718) 265-FISH

The aquarium is the only aquatic attraction in Brooklyn that doesn't require cement boots. Going anywhere that dealt with "the fish" was not a good thing in my world. Thank goodness my only visit with the fish in Brooklyn was not at the bottom of Gravesend Bay but at the lively New York Aquarium. There's a huge difference between the Brooklyn underworld I knew and the aquarium's underwater world, offered year round.

During the summer months, wait till you see the dolphins perform. Much smarter than most of the thugs I dealt with, including me. Find yourself suddenly on the West Coast in the Sea Cliffs area. It's a rocky shore doubling for the Pacific Northwest where visitors can explore tidal pools and crashing-wave rock formations.

Coney Island USA
1208 Surf Avenue
Brooklyn
(718) 372-5159

Yes, Coney Island the park is still here and catering to youngsters as it has for decades. If your kids are freaks, they'll fit right in. There are historical exhibits on the park as well as current amusements including the Cyclone Roller Coaster. Make sure to stop by Nathan's for a dog.

Empire State Building Observatory
350 Fifth Avenue at 34th Street
Manhattan
(212) 736-3100

No kid's visit to New York is complete without going up to the 86th-floor observation deck of the same building that big ape

climbed. Even without the youngsters, this is one romantic spot.
There was the Tom Hanks and Meg
Ryan finale in the movie *Sleepless in
Seattle*. Remember *An Affair to Remember?* To this day you can find
modern-day Cary Grants waiting
for their Deborah Kerrs. The
building has seventy miles of water pipe and 2,500,000 feet of
wire, and you know the mob
taxed every inch of it.

This is me as a cocky little wiseguy. Coney
Island.

FDNY Fire Zone

34 West 51st Street
Manhattan
(212) 698-4520

The best way for kids to learn important stuff on fire safety and
have a good time doing so. They learn how to stop fires and how
not to start them. Some of my associates should have paid a visit
here. Well, we knew how to start them.

Rockefeller Center

Spans 48th to 51st Streets between Fifth Avenue
*   and the Avenue of the Americas*
Manhattan

I can't think of a more beautiful place over the holidays. Rockefeller Center is home to the famous Christmas tree and ice-skating
rink. It's also home to romantic couples and families visiting from
all over the globe.

Zoos

For some reason, my mobster pals loved animals, maybe because
we were "animals" ourselves. My friend Brooksy had a chimp. We

used to take him to bars with us. He was a hit. Brooksy really liked his chimpanzee. Can't remember the name. Nice chimp, though. Guys had other animals for other reasons. Crazy Joe Gallo had two lions in his basement. Let's just say they weren't because Joe was lonely and liked to go in his basement. I think Joe was a prick to those poor cats, and they should have eaten him.

Bronx Zoo

Fordham Road at the Bronx River Parkway
Bronx (take exit 6 on the Bronx River Parkway)
(718) 367-1010

This is one old zoo, an oldie but a goodie. It's the largest metro-zoo in the country, tough to see it all in one day. The Bronx Zoo opened in 1899 and has been a family favorite ever since. Kids can enjoy a real Congo experience or the ever-popular World of Reptiles exhibit. Even Mafia families enjoyed the lion cages as a disposal venue for soon-to-be-devoured men who crossed them. This isn't some urban legend. I heard a story in 1971 about this guy I knew, Tony "Smiley" Rosato. Crazy fuck thought everything was funny. "Hey Tony, I just lost a lot on that game." The prick would just laugh. "Say, Tony, I spotted your goumada with some punk at the airport, his mitts all over her." Still, he'd just laugh the shit off. Then he tried to skate on a way-overdue loan shark debt. With those sharks, the longer you blow the payments off, the sooner you get blown away. To the zoo Smiley went. The lion house to be exact. I wonder if he was laughing when that lioness grabbed him by the back of the neck.

The Bronx Zoo was one of the first to take the animals out of cages and into a more natural habitat. The property is responsible for breeding endangered breeds for the survival of the species. It began the kind of stuff you always hear the San Diego Zoo getting credit for. Breeding and no cages: I wish they brought that philosophy to us mob animals all the times I was locked up. The exhibits are terrific. Be sure to check out the African Plains, World of Darkness, Wild Asia, and the Aquatic Bird House. This goes without saying, leave plenty of time for the Monkey House. The Congo Gorilla Forest is amazing, informative, and huge.

Hungry (and thirsty) zoo-goers should hit the Flamingo Pub. Summer is the best season, but it's also the most crowded, and since the zoo is open year-round, you can go anytime you visit the city.

Central Park Zoo
830 Fifth Avenue
Manhattan
(212) 861-6030

These animals boast the most expensive zip code of the animal kingdom. You can check out species from the steamy jungles to the polar icecaps, all between shopping at Saks Fifth Avenue and seeing a Broadway show.

Prospect Park Zoo
450 Flatbush Avenue
Brooklyn
(718) 399-7339

Gangster Trivia

Bootlegging spawned the modern wiseguys.

When I was a kid, I remember farms in Brooklyn. We'd get fresh milk, fresh eggs, and the smell of fresh horse droppings. Nowadays, the only animals in Brooklyn are mobsters and those found at the Prospect Park Zoo/Wildlife Center. The animals at Prospect Park are cuter and better behaved.

Check out the baboons for a close resemblance to my old buddies. All kids should have the chance to experience the interactive section of the zoo. This permits the youngsters to actually get into the animal's world, cleverly titled the World of Animals.

Make sure to attend the Annual Fleece Festival in late April, where you can still spend a day on a farm in Brooklyn. There's music and games as well as sheep getting their yearly visit from the local barber.

Queens Zoo

53-51 111th Street
Flushing Meadows, Corona Park, Queens
(718) 271-1500

The Mafia had those members that were Italian-born and then those of us who were born here in the United States. The older guys came from the old country. My generation, for the most part, grew up in Brooklyn or Queens. We were the majority in the organization by the time I was in it. As far as the other animals go, the Queens Zoo is an All-American Zoo, meaning the animals are native to North or South America. You got your bears, elk, mountain lions, donkeys, bison, and plenty more great wildlife from this continent.

Queens Wildlife Center Sheep-Shearing Weekend

53-51 111th Street
Queens
(718) 271-7761

Late April. Anything sporting hair within a stone's throw of the Queens Wildlife Center, excluding the rats and homeless, go to the animal barber this weekend for their annual haircuts.

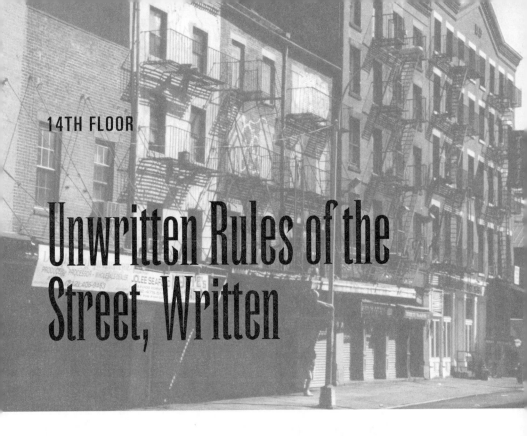

Unwritten Rules of the Street, Written

The scariest part about being around so many people is you never know who's suddenly going to kill you. Better yet, you might have some pride and start some shit and learn some little old fart is actually kicking your ass. "Father Time," as we'll refer to him, was a loanshark in with the Lucchese organization. Watch out, no matter how old he got, he could still kick your ass. He had this huge Rolex that I swear was so damn heavy he could barely lift his arm. When it came time to collect, or someone rubbed him the wrong way, this watch came off and became a plated yellow gold knuckle. You wouldn't believe how many guys had this look of shock just before they got smashed again. Only in New York does this stuff happen daily. It's a rough world inside a rough world.

The "streets" is the universal term for the urban outdoors. The meaning goes way beyond the actual streets. If you spend too much time on the actual streets, a cab will flatten you. The "streets" include alleys, sidewalks, doorsteps, underpasses, sewers, subways, and parks. New York's streets are very dangerous.

The city's shined up so much since my day because of the hard work of good people. Nope, I can't take any credit for that. Still nothing can stop the capable numbers of frustrated, greedy, evil, crazy, dangerous people waiting to mug, rape, rob, murder, scare, or eat you. Just make sure you pack you wits, common sense, some mace, and a .38 before your visit, and you should be fine (unless you turned states' evidence on a large number of New York mobsters). Stay in groups. If you're alone and it's late, make friends. Steer clear of dark alleys and dark characters. Don't go creeping around warehouses, and many of the addresses in this book you should explore only during daylight hours. Don't ask questions except for directions out of there. Following are some tips and terms that might be useful in guiding you smoothly through the underworld.

Death Prevention Tips

There's nothing like coming home alive from a visit to New York City. Unfortunately, "murder" and "New York City" are two things often found in the same sentence. Murder rates have dropped significantly lately, but that's not to say dead-weight bodies still don't drop to the ground regularly. They just don't do it as often. Murderers love tourists, because tourists don't have New York home addresses or many local friends or family. To a bad guy, the most exciting thing about tourists is they are gullible and usually carrying a lot of money.

1. Don't ask some rough looking bastard which Mafia family he belongs to. Dumb move. Don't waltz into an Italian restaurant I recommend in this book and tell them you expect to see some real-life Tony Sopranos and then start reciting Pesci's lines from *Goodfellas.* You might die, and you will have your food á la lugie. Just mind your fucking business and enjoy the best food on earth.

2. Refrain from going to areas off the beaten path, especially at night. If you do, don't give directions, answer questions, or pull out a map. The 911 emergency number works good in New York.

3. Don't get any hookers and don't tease any pimps.

4. Never walk into a "social club" or "members only" business.

If guys like this come toward you, don't make eye contact.

5. Unless it's Halloween, don't wear weird shit like headbands, bandanas, or cycling shorts.

6. Don't hop in some half-ass questionable "car service" for a ride. Stick to the yellow cabs, and the ride won't be your last.

7. If someone stumbles in front of you, kick them. It's a setup.

8. Don't allow yourself to be coaxed into an alley for a free "Broadway show" ticket.

9. Don't carry a gun. Guns provoke guns. Better off with a good pair of running sneakers (with knife-toes).

10. Don't get too trashed.

11. Don't get too trashed, especially if you ignore Tips 5 and 9.

Mugging/Robbery Prevention Tips

If you're a tourist, you gotta realize there are assholes in New York that want to rob you. They're waiting for you. I want to share some of the quotes I've heard in my days in the city. Welcome to New

Italian influence.

York. "Give me your wallet and watch now, mother fucker, now!" Welcome to New York. "Your purse, bitch, your purse, bitch!" Welcome to New York. "Don't make me do this, I'll do it." They pick pockets, swipe purses, and get your shoes. Your basic urban jerks. There are proven tricks and tactics against these assholes:

1. Women, don't wear lots of visible jewelry out on the town.

2. Men, don't wear women's jewelry, period.

3. Don't keep your wallet in the "sucker" pocket. If you're not sure which pocket that is, it's the back pocket, sucker! Keep everything in your front pockets. At restaurants, don't leave your purse on the back of the chair. When carrying it, wear it with the strap across your chest.

4. If possible, always keep in groups. The more the merrier, the less the scarier. Why? Hell, I've lost count of the number of times I've heard of guys and girls getting popped, mugged,

and raped (mostly girls) without witnesses. Usually the only witness is the fucker jumping you.

5. If someone tells you, "You have ketchup on your coat," don't look down to wipe it off. You're about to get popped. Another old one is, some fuck claims you dropped money. Don't let your guard down and bend over to get it. Just roll, buddy.

6. On subways, buses, and benches, keep your briefcase or purse on your lap. If you have a girlfriend, keep her on your lap.

7. Don't count money outside. Don't show money, period.

8. Don't pull out maps in public. Ask police or metro folks for directions. Always check your humble watch confidently, as if you are on your way somewhere. Talk the talk and walk the walk. New Yorkers are always in hurry. Get in a hurry, too, even if you're not, you'll blend in.

Gangster Trivia

Carmine Galante's nephew, bearing the same name, was on the television show America's Most Wanted in 1999 at age twenty-two, for the alleged murder of an eighteen-year-old college student in a Bay Ridge bar.

9. Bring your drugs to New York, even FedEx them to the hotel. It's safer than trying to score drugs off the street. For a tourist, buying drugs is a great way to get killed.

10. Do not answer your hotel room door unless you know who it is. Do not answer anyone for that matter.

The Wiseguy Top Ten

Disclaimer: *Do not take the following lists literally.* Although they come from years of experience, trial and error, this guide is meant

Brooklyn and Queens are packed with "fine Italian cuisine" as seen here.

to be a humorous take on the subject, not an actual guide for killing, robbing, intimidating, maiming, or causing discomfort to yourself and others.

LEAVE AN IMPRESSION

Someone owes you, but if you whack 'em, you're gonna get squat. Sometimes you need to wise them up a bit to get paid.

10. Head Cheese. Shave their head and massage it with a cheese grater.

9. Il Soffio di Naso. Stuff a ladyfinger (or similar explosive) up the nose or duct-tape an M-80 under the nose and light fuse.

8. Van GoGo. Slice off both ears of the offending person.

7. Shaky Shake. Cut deeply across the palm of your adversary's dominant hand with a rusty knife so they can make no business deals in the near future without a shaky shake.

6. The Gimp. Cutting the Achilles tendon results in years of limping.

5. Manhattan Rodeo. Tie a gagged, unconscious victim under a parked car behind a nightclub. Within a couple hours, the rodeo begins.

4. Zipper Mouth. Needs to have a good set of teeth. Tie the enemy down, and with precision, knock out every other top tooth, and do the same to the bottom teeth. The goal is to have the look of one row when jaws are closed.

3. Microwaved Weiner. Stick a pair of closed needle-nosed pliers about an inch and a half up the guy's peehole and suddenly spread them.

2. Devil's Smile. Force your victim to kiss a hot grill or pan for five to ten seconds—the lips will peel back and bleed for weeks.

1. Pipe Cleaner. Make 'em swallow a mouse and sit on a piece of cheese.

Mafia's Top-Ten Hits

The Mafia has historically come up with new and innovative ways of taking another's life. In my day there were a few rules (one being no car bombs, which was broken from time to time). The following are my favorites, some I witnessed and some I heard about.

"I dug the hole last time. You dig it."

10. Squirmer. Bury them alive after a beating. The victim will often squirm until sufficient dirt is displaced to finish the job.

9. Steak House Ambush. Surprise and shoot or stab the

target at a restaurant, preferably with their family and friends present.

8. Copper Migraine. Use a .22-caliber with long copper bullet behind the ear.

7. Brooklyn Fogger. Place a plastic bag over the head.

6. Sicilian Neck Tie. Slice the throat.

5. Bad Starter. Wire a car bomb to the ignition.

4. Garrote. Cut the throat with a piano wire.

3. The Yankee Clipper. Baseball-bat the person to death while taunting.

2. White Shotgun. Give a shotgun blast to the face so that an open-casket funeral is impossible.

1. Brain Picker. Abruptly hammer or thrust an ice pick through the skull.

Best Ways to Hide a Corpse

Many say they are more worried about how to get rid of the body once it's dead than the killing itself. Here are some gruesome ways to hide a body.

10. Sewer Rat. Simple: Dump the corpse in the sewer.

9. Waste Management. Just toss the body in a dumpster.

8. Italian Oven. Combine mid-summer heat, the dead body, and the trunk of an abandoned car.

7. Cement Boots. A classic.

6. Rubber Ducky. Leave the naked, trash-bagged corpse in the enemy's home bathtub.

5. Scrap Yard Graveyard. Stack several bodies in a trunk and have the car compacted.

4. Construction-Site Casket. Bury the victim deep in cement.

Gangster Trivia

3. Scatter Technique. Dismember into burlap bags and spread along the Jersey Turnpike.

2. Coney Island Foot Long. Make sure you have access to the local meat processing plant and don't eat franks for a while.

When you finally learn the game, you realize you shouldn't be playing. It's a one-way ticket.

1. Sack of Lime. Bury the body at least four feet under and cover it with lime to quickly dissolve the remains and hide the stench.

Don't let these lists scare you. The city is the best in the world and worth your visit. Use caution but don't let fear get too much in the way of the adventure. If you get hurt, don't blame me, but I think every trip should have a little trouble. It makes for a better story when you get home.

I N D E X